Life is what you make it

PETER BUFFETT

Life is what you make it

HARMONY BOOKS • NEW YORK

Published in the United States by Harmony Books,
an imprint of the Crown Publishing Group,
a division of Random House, Inc., New York.
www.crownpublishing.com

Grateful acknowledgment is made to Taylor Mali for
permission to use an excerpt from "What Teachers Make" from
What Learning Leaves by Taylor Mali (Hanover Press, 2002),
copyright © 2002 by Taylor Mali.

Library of Congress Cataloging-in-Publication Data
Buffett, Peter.
Life is what you make it / Peter Buffett.—1st ed.
p. cm.
1. Buffett, Peter. 2. Buffett, Warren—Family. 3. Conduct of life.
4. Values. 5. Children of the rich—United States—Biography.
6. Composers—United States—Biography. I. Title.
BJ1581.2.B773 2010
158—dc22 2009030927

ISBN 978-0-307-46471-2

Printed in the United States of America

DESIGN BY BARBARA STURMAN

2 4 6 8 10 9 7 5 3 1

First Edition

This book is dedicated to
my mother and father

The privilege of a lifetime is being who you are.

—JOSEPH CAMPBELL

Contents

Life is what you make it

Introduction

This is a book about gifts received and gifts given back to the world, about expectations and obligations, about family and community, and how they shape us. It's about living in a society that lulls us with unprecedented comforts, but also tweaks us with anxieties—both economic and otherwise—and too often leaves us empty and bewildered in our search for purpose.

In short, this is a book about values—about the convictions and intuitions that define what's worth doing during our brief stay on Earth, about the actions and attitudes that will add up to a well-lived life. Economic prosperity may come and go; that's just how it is. But values are the steady currency that earn us the all-important rewards of self-respect and peace of mind.

This is also a book about identity—about the callings and talents and decisions and quirks that make each of us uniquely who we are.

Values and identity. In my view, these things can be meaningfully addressed only as two sides of the same coin. Our values guide our choices; our choices define who we are. *Life is what we make it.* The concept is simple, but the process by which we make our own lives can be complex and baffling. Expectations and external pressures blur the outline of our truest selves. Economic reality, for good or ill, plays a big role in the dynamic, as does pure dumb luck.

Ultimately, though, we create the lives we live. This is our greatest burden and greatest opportunity. It is also the most basic, bedrock premise of everything I have to say in these pages.

So then, what sort of people will we choose to be? In the myriad choices that we face each day, will we choose the path of least resistance—or the path of potentially greatest satisfaction? In our dealings with others, will we meekly shy away from intimacy and honesty and tolerance—or will we open ourselves to robust and candid relationships? In our work lives, will we settle for making a living—no sure thing these days!—or aim at the higher goal of earning a life? How will we become worthy of the various gifts we have received? How will we learn the redemptive art of giving back?

Answers to these questions can come only from inside

each of us. The goal of this book is simply to raise them, to offer a framework for thought and, I hope, discussion.

But who am I to be writing such a book? The honest answer is *no one in particular*. I'm not a trained philosopher or sociologist, and I'm not setting up shop as one more self-help guru. My only credential, in fact, is my own life—a life that has forced me to think long and hard about these matters.

By the luck of the draw—what my father calls "winning the Ovarian Lottery"—I was born into a caring and supportive family, a family whose first and most important gift to me was emotional security. Over time, as a bonus that came as a gradual and wonderful surprise, my family also got to be wealthy and distinguished. My dad, Warren Buffett, by dint of hard work, solid ethics, and steady wisdom, has become one of the richest and most respected men in the world. I say this with plenty of filial pride—but also with the humble acknowledgment that those are *his* accomplishments, not mine. No matter who your parents are, you've still got your own life to figure out.

Further, as is widely known, my father has some pretty strong opinions on the subject of inherited wealth. Basically, he believes that the silver spoon in the mouth too often becomes the silver dagger in the back—an ill-considered gift that saps ambition and drains motivation, that deprives a young person of the great adventure of finding his or her own way. My father had the enormous satisfaction of discovering his own passion and making his own mark; why should his kids be denied that challenge and that pleasure? So, no big trust funds for the Buffett clan! My siblings and I, upon turning nineteen, were each given a very modest amount of money, with the clear understanding that we should expect no more.

Certainly there would be no juicy end-of-life bequests. Back in 2006, my father, in an act of philanthropy historic in its scale, gave away the bulk of his fortune—$37 billion—to the Bill and Melinda Gates Foundation. At the same time, he established billion-dollar charitable endowments to be administered by each of his three children.

So here's an irony for you. Today, at the age of fifty, I find myself with the enormous opportunity and responsibility of stewardship over a billion dollars meant to be given away, while in my own mind I remain very much a working stiff—a composer and musician who, like most of my colleagues, is only as good as his last composition, neither more nor less successful than my next job lets me be.

But that's okay; I'm doing something I love, something I've chosen for myself, and I wouldn't have it any other way. I guess I've inherited more than just my father's genes; I seem to have absorbed much of his philosophy as well.

Don't get me wrong: I am very well aware that I was born into a privileged life. The economic head start I received from my father may have been a relatively modest one, but still, it was more than most people have—and it was entirely unearned. Similarly, through no merit of my own, I have enjoyed the various, often intangible benefits of a famous last name. Far from denying these advantages, I have spent my life wrestling with their meaning and implications and consequences. To stand an old cliché on its head, I've had to learn to make the best of a good situation.

There is a famous quotation from the Book of Luke that was taken very seriously in our family: *From those to whom much has been given, much is expected.* And it was made very clear that the most important gifts of all had nothing to do with money. There were the gifts of parental love and close community and warm friendship, of inspiring teachers and mentors who took delight in our development. There were the mysterious gifts of talent and competence, capacity for empathy and hard work. These gifts were meant to be respected and repaid.

But how? How do we repay the gifts that came to us unbidden and more or less at random? And not just repay them, but *amplify* them, so that they grow beyond our own small circle to make a difference in the world? How do we balance ambition and service, personal goals and the common good? How do we avoid the pressures that can trap us into lives that are not really our own? How can we work toward a version of success that we define for ourselves—

a success based on values and substance, rather than mere dollars and the approval of others, and that cannot be tarnished or taken away by shifting fashions or a bad economy?

It is my belief, based both on intuition and observation, that there are many, many people wrestling with these questions. Young men and women hankering to set off on their own course, even when their aspirations entail risk and sacrifice and bold divergence from the usual paths. Parents who want to instill solid values in their kids, so that they grow up with a sense of gratitude and adventure, rather than the smug passivity that comes from feeling entitled.

These people, and many others—teachers, nurses, business leaders, artists—recognize that they are members of a society unprecedented in its affluence but appalling in its inequality. They are people of conscience—people who respect the gifts that they've been given and want to use those gifts to make not just a livelihood, but a difference. If this book is of some small help and comfort to the many individuals who are questing to live their own true lives, and to give back in the process, then I will have accomplished what I hoped to do.

1

Normal is what you're used to

You're Warren Buffett's son? But you seem so normal!

Over the course of my life, I have heard many versions of this comment, and I have always taken it as a compliment—a compliment not to me, but to my family.

Why? Because what we mean by "normal" really comes down to this: that a person can function effectively and find acceptance among other human beings. To put it another way, it means that a person has been given the best possible chance to make the most of his or her own life.

This ability, in turn, can come only from an embrace of the social and emotional values that connect us all. And those values are learned—maybe it would be more accurate to say *absorbed*—at home.

Those core values are the foundation for everything I

have to say in this book. So let's look a little more closely at a few of them, and consider how they are passed along.

Very near the top of the list, I would place the concept of "trust." Taken in the very widest sense, trust is the belief that the world is a good place. Not a perfect place, as anyone can see, but a good place—and a place worth the trouble of trying to make better. If you want to function effectively in the world—not to mention stay in a good mood—this is a very useful thing to believe!

Trust in the world is inseparable from a trust in people—a belief that human beings, however flawed we all are, are fundamentally well-intentioned. People want to do the right thing. Clearly, there are many pitfalls and temptations that lead people to do the wrong thing. But doing the wrong thing is a perversion, a betrayal of our true nature. Our true nature is to be fair and kind.

Not everyone believes this, of course. Some people think that human beings are fundamentally bad—grasping, competitive, inclined to lie and cheat. Frankly, I feel sorry for people who see it that way. It must be difficult for them to get through the day—to maintain open friendships, to do business without constant scheming and suspicion, even to love.

The belief—the faith—that people are basically good

is one of the core values that allow us to feel at home in the world.

Where does this all-important trust come from? It has to start with a loving family then extends outward to a caring and secure community.

I was very fortunate in my upbringing. In our famously mobile society, my family was remarkably stable. The house I grew up in—a very average, early-twentieth-century-subdivision sort of house that my father had bought in 1958 for $31,500!—was two blocks from where my mother had grown up. My grandparents still lived there. The city of Omaha was filling in around us, and the neighborhood became a strange mix of rural and urban. Our street was actually a main artery going in and out of town, but our house was rather barn-like, with teardrop attic windows like those seen in *The Amityville Horror.* Just for the fun of it, we used to plant a few rows of corn in our small side yard.

As soon as I proved that I was able to look both ways before crossing the street, I was allowed to walk by myself to visit my grandparents. The space between my parents' and my grandparents' houses was like a bubble or corridor of love. I got hugs at both ends of the journey. My grandmother was an archetype of a perhaps vanishing breed: a homemaker, and proud of it. She was always cooking, running errands, or doing projects around the house. When I appeared, she made me ice-cream cones with little candy surprises embedded in every scoop. My grandfather always wanted to know what I'd learned in school that day. On the walk back home, neighbors would wave or toot their horns.

Idyllic? Sure. And I am only too aware that not every child has the benefit of such a serene and supportive home environment. Those that don't have that benefit have a lot more ground to cover on the path of learning to trust the world.

But the point I'd like to make here is this: The things that allowed me to feel safe and trusting as a kid had nothing to do with money or material advantages.

It didn't matter how big our house was; it mattered that there was love in it. It didn't matter if our neighborhood was wealthy or otherwise; it mattered that neighbors talked to each other, looked out for one another. The kindnesses that allowed me to trust in people and in the basic goodness of the world could not be measured in dollars; they were paid for, rather, in hugs and ice-cream cones and help with homework.

They were kindnesses that every parent and every community should be able to shower on their children.

If trust is the core value that allows us to meet the world in a cheerful stance, then *tolerance* is the equally important quality that allows us to deal with the realities of differences and conflict. Let's be honest: If people were all more or less the same—if there were no differences in race, religion, sexual orientation, political leanings—life would in some ways be easier. But, boy, would it be dull! Diversity is the spice of life. Our ability to embrace diversity makes our own lives richer.

Conversely, whenever we fall victim to prejudice or unadmitted bias, we make our own lives smaller and poorer. You don't believe that women are the equal of men in the workplace? Well, your world has just shrunk by half. You have a problem with gay people? Well, you just deprived yourself of 10 percent of the population. You're not comfortable with black people? Latinos? You get my drift. Keep giving in to intolerance, and eventually your world contains no one but you and a few people who look like you and think like you; it gets to resemble a small, snooty, and deathly dull country club! Is that a world worth living in?

Tolerance was one of the key values I absorbed at home. I'm proud to say that my parents were actively engaged in the civil rights struggles of the late fifties and early sixties. I was just a child at the time—much too young to understand the complexity and awful history behind the issues of the day. But I didn't need to be lectured about racism and bigotry; all I had to do was keep my eyes open.

My mother, who was never shy about letting people know where she stood, had a bumper sticker on her car that said NICE PEOPLE COME IN ALL COLORS. One morning we found that someone had crossed out ALL COLORS and scrawled in WHITE. This petty and stupid bit of vandalism was a revelation to me. Racism was something that happened—or so I'd thought—far away, in places like Selma, Alabama, and that we watched on television news reports. But this was Omaha—supposedly a bastion of fair-mindedness and common sense—and racism was here as well.

This was hugely disappointing, but I learned a couple things from it. First, that one should never take tolerance for granted, but work actively to foster it. Second, that the smug belief that prejudice is someone else's failing—in this case, that of the benighted Southerners—is itself a kind of bias. Plenty of us Midwesterners shared the taint.

If racism has provided the most dramatic test of tolerance in my lifetime, it certainly isn't the only arena where there is ground to be covered and lessons to be learned.

My mother was also determined to imbue us with religious tolerance. When I was a teenager, she would take me to different churches, so I could experience various modes of worship. We went to a Southern Baptist church in which a minister stirred up the congregation to a fever pitch with his scriptural interpretations; women in white uniforms stood in the aisles, ready to catch and attend to those who fainted from ecstasy. We went to a synagogue whose unfamiliar language and ancient rituals gave rise to a different but equal kind of awe. At home we had books about the great Eastern religions, Buddhism and Hinduism.

The constant lesson was that each of these belief systems was a sincere and valid approach to the spiritual. None of them was "right." None of them was "wrong." They were human—and therefore approximate and incomplete—attempts to connect with the Divine. All were worthy of respect. Far from dividing people, my mother believed, religion should make people allies in their shared quest for meaning and transcendence.

She was so constant and passionate in her fostering of tolerance that I took to calling her the Dalai Mama. If she could have taken her teaching to the Middle East (and if anyone had listened), the world would be a much more peaceful place today!

These family attitudes about religion and race were part of a more general emphasis on the importance of open-mindedness. One should *always* show respect to other people and dissenting opinions. One should *always* try to understand the opposite side of an argument. This was a moral imperative but also an intellectual one: Grasping an opposing point of view was a way of sharpening the mind.

My mother had been on the debating team in high school. She reveled in spirited but civil discussion, and the Buffett kitchen was a lively place.

My older brother, Howie, was also a debater. This

caused me much frustration growing up. In our family discussions, he always seemed more nimble, more persuasive. He knew more words! Words like *nevertheless* and *conversely*. But if I often felt outmaneuvered and outreasoned in these family debates, I also learned a valuable lesson—a lesson that allowed me to feel more confident and more relaxed in these discussions (and even arguments!): No one *wins* a conversation, and no one loses.

You can win a tennis match. You can lose a baseball game. Discussions aren't like that. The purpose is to exchange ideas, to gauge the merits of different points of view. If anything, the person who "loses" the battle of words has actually "won"—since he or she has learned more from the transaction.

This brings me to another of my family's core values: a fervent belief in education.

A distinction is in order. Much of what is called "education" these days, even at the college level, is in fact more in the nature of job-training. A particular major is a ticket to a particular degree, which in turn is a ticket to a particular career. Now, as a practical person, I'm not knocking this. If your ambition is to be an investment banker or a management consultant, then, sure, an MBA is the likeliest way to get there. Majoring in poli sci as a prelude to law school makes perfect sense.

But my point is that this relatively narrow, goal-oriented sort of learning is only one aspect of what education really means—and not the most important aspect, either. Life is what we make it, and if we want our lives to be as rich and round and gratifying as possible, we should try to learn about *everything*—not just what we need to know to make our livings, but all the innumerable subjects at the periphery of our specialties.

Book-learning is certainly a part—a wonderful part—of this broader education. This is a conviction I absorbed mainly from observing my grandfather, who showed me how much serenity and joy there could be in sitting quietly with a book. I can still picture him relaxing in his La-Z-Boy, his pants almost up to his chin, his teeth, as likely as not, in a glass at his side! He was the scholar of the family, and it was his influence that led me, for example, to study Latin in junior high school.

Was there any *use* in studying Latin? Not really. But it was a nice thing to know, a link to history and to the traditions of our culture. In other words, it was part of education for education's sake. And doing my Latin homework at my grandfather's side—the two of us turning to the back of the book to look up the words we didn't know—was a wonderful exercise in family bonding.

I think of education, ultimately, as the fulfillment of curiosity. One of the best things parents can do for their children, therefore, is to keep that curiosity stoked. In our household, this was accomplished by wide-ranging conversation and the frequent advice to *look it up*. When I had questions, when some discussion or school project cried out for further information, I was steered to our family copy of the *World Book Encyclopedia* or to our vast archive of back issues of *National Geographic*.

I should add that, back in those pre-Google days, when one searched for something, one really searched! As a kid, I spent a lot of time on my hands and knees, looking for the magazine that had the article "Birds of East Africa" or "Peoples of the Amazon." Doing research was a treasure hunt. As with any hunt, there was suspense and adventure in the process, and appreciation and fulfillment when the treasure was finally found. A few clicks in a search-box might be more efficient, but it may not be as satisfying. I often ended up taking volumes of the encyclopedia to bed with me just to read for fun. The short passages about people, places, or things would fascinate me to no end.

Another way in which my family stressed the value of education was by taking an active interest in my school. Too many parents, I think, regard their kids' schools as mysterious brick boxes into which their children disappear from eight to three each day, but which don't have a lot to do with *them*. As long as the report cards are okay, as long as no discipline problems are reported, these sorts of parents stay largely aloof. Oh, sure, there's the occasional visiting day or parent-teacher conference, but too often these are mere formalities—if not downright torture for all concerned!

My mother saw it differently. She would sometimes show up at my elementary school and even high school. (She knew her way around. They'd been her schools, too!) She would just sit quietly at the back of the room, observing the class, seeing what was being taught, and how. Her level of interest made me proud, and made me understand that my schooling was important. It wasn't a matter of the grades I brought home a few times a year, but of what I was actually learning from day to day. If more parents showed that degree of involvement with their children's education, I think that more kids would get through school with their intellectual curiosity and appetite for learning intact.

Schooling and book-learning are important parts of education, of course; but in my view, they are not the most essential parts. Sure, for technical things like physics or statistics, there is no substitute for formal study. But looked at from a broader perspective—the perspective of making our lives as rich and rewarding as they can possibly be—books and schools may be the tools of education, but they are not its substance.

The substance of education has to do with understanding human nature—both our own inmost hearts, and the motives and longings of people very different from ourselves. That kind of education doesn't come from encyclopedias or dusty old magazines or even Google. It comes from respectful engagement with a wide range of other people. It comes from careful listening.

Of all the ways in which my mother impressed upon me the value of education, maybe the most profound is this: She taught me that everyone had a story worth listening to. This is another way of saying that everyone has something to teach.

During my childhood, my mother was determined to acquaint me with as many people and as many stories as possible. When I was very young, we hosted exchange students from several African countries. We had a Czech student stay with us for a time. There were always visitors at our house from another side of town or another side of the world. Sometimes, coming home from elementary school for lunch, I would find my mother deep in conversation with a guest from Africa or Europe. My mother would usually be probing in her gentle but incisive manner. What was life like where they lived? What were the difficulties, the struggles? What were their ambitions and their dreams? What did they believe in?

Even before I was equipped to grasp the answers, I absorbed the lesson that these were the important questions.

I want to touch on one more core value I learned from my family. In terms of earning self-respect, it might be the most important of them all, and I am especially indebted to my father for leading me to see its importance.

I'm referring to the development of a personal work ethic.

But let's take a moment to define what the Buffett family work ethic is—and, equally important, what it *isn't*.

Some people believe that having a good work ethic equates with a willingness to slave away for sixty or eighty hours a week, at a job for which one has no passion or even actively hates. The idea here is that the sheer effort, self-denial, and time logged on the clock are somehow intrinsically virtuous.

But excuse me—that's not virtue; it's masochism! In some cases it's also, paradoxically, a sign of laziness and lack of imagination. If you're such a hard worker, why not use some of that effort and some of those hours to find something you actually *like*?

For my father—and now for me—the essence of a good work ethic starts with meeting a challenge of self-discovery, finding something you love to do, so that work—even, or especially, when it is very difficult and arduous—becomes joyful, maybe even sacred.

When I was very young, my father mostly worked at home. He spent long hours in his office—a small, hushed room off of my parents' bedroom—studying massive and mysterious books. These, I later learned, were things like Value Line and Moody's—detailed statistical analyses of thousands of companies and their stocks. But if the subjects my father studied were essentially pragmatic, the concentration that he brought to the process bordered on the mystical. His "scripture" might have consisted of things like price-to-earnings ratios and breakdowns of management performance, but he could as easily have been a rabbi studying Kabbalah or a Buddhist monk puzzling over Zen *koans*. His focus was that fierce—that pure. It is only a slight exaggeration to say that when my father was working, he went into an altered state, a trance. He'd emerge from his office, wearing his usual outfit of khaki pants and a worn-out sweater, and there would be an almost saintly calm about him—the calm of a person whose ego has completely merged with the task at hand.

It is a well-known fact that extreme physical effort promotes the release of substances called endorphins—natural feel-good compounds with the power to blot out pain, make time seem to slow down, and give rise to a blissful state of well-being. My father's affect when he was deep in work suggested that extreme *mental* effort released endorphins, too. Observing him at these times, I learned a simple but profound lesson. I learned that work should be demanding and intense—*and that it should make us happy.*

What was it about my father's approach to work that allowed him to remain so unremittingly cheerful in the face of long hours and wearying decisions? First and foremost, it was that he really wasn't doing it for the money. Eventually, the money came—and that was a very gratifying confirmation of the wisdom of his approach to business. But the money was a by-product, an afterthought. What mattered was the *substance* of the work: exercising his boundless curiosity, testing his analyses against real-world performance, living the adventure of discovering value and new possibilities.

If my father had been working mainly for the money, his efforts would have quickly dulled into a routine—a job. What has kept him sharp and engaged for all these years is the intellectual challenge, the serious and consequential game. That part of it is new every day.

This leads me to another observation about some people's mistaken notions of what a good work ethic really is.

Some people *think* they're talking about a work ethic, when what they're really talking about is a *wealth* ethic. They claim to have a high regard for labor and discipline and perseverance, but those qualities are not what they truly respect; what they respect is the wealth those qualities sometimes lead to. They honor the payoff rather than the process.

There are all sorts of moral and philosophical arguments that could be made against this inversion of values. But I'd like to offer a purely practical objection: The problem with honoring the rewards of work rather than the work itself is that the rewards can always be taken away.

All of us who've been living through dicey economic times know this only too well. Is a person a success one day and a failure the next simply because, through no fault of her own, her firm goes out of business? Is a brilliant entrepreneur suddenly a loser because conditions change in worldwide markets?

Why would people wager their self-respect on factors so far out of their control?

A sane and durable work ethic keeps the emphasis not on fickle rewards, but on the work itself—on the passion and focus and seriousness of purpose with which the work is approached.

Those are the things that no one can take away from us.

2

No one deserves anything

No one asks to be born.

No one gets to choose his parents or to have a say in the circumstances of her birth.

A life may begin in a snug and comfortable bedroom in an American suburb or on a straw mat in a mud hut in West Africa. The parents could be residents of a Park Avenue penthouse, or homeless people barely surviving in a public park. They might be healthy, or they might be infected with HIV. They could be athletes and scholars, or crack addicts and criminals. They could be partners in a committed couple for whom parenthood will be one of life's high points, or they could be virtual strangers out on a date, completely indifferent to the consequences of their actions.

The range of possibilities is practically limitless, and these happenstances of birth will of course affect those new lives in profound and complicated ways. But allow me to state something that, while obvious, is often conveniently overlooked.

People born to good parents in advantageous circumstances don't deserve any credit for the situation. On the other hand, people born to bad parents and in poverty don't deserve any blame. How could they? We aren't even innocent bystanders, let alone active coconspirators, as our particular birth-lottery is playing out; we don't even exist yet!

Clearly, then, at the start of our lives, no one deserves anything. No one *deserves* to be rich or poor, privileged or oppressed, healthy or challenged. No one *deserves* good parents or bad. These are things that happen randomly to the life that has just begun. They are neither fair nor unfair; they simply *are*.

This randomness is a little hard to swallow. At one end of the luck continuum, those who've gotten a bad shake at the start of life tend to feel an understandable but unproductive resentment, a bitter suspicion that the universe is not their friend. At the good-luck end of the spectrum, something even stranger often takes place. Against all reason, against the most fundamental rules of logic, people believe they were born wealthy or good-looking because they *deserved* to be born wealthy or good-looking. Clearly, this makes no sense, but people tend to believe it anyway. It's flattering.

We will in due course consider the motives and the consequences of this false belief. For right now, let's just let the illogic speak for itself.

The truth is that, at the start of life, randomness rules. Accepting this is, I believe, the beginning of humility, and also the starting point for a realistic approach to making the most of the one life that each of us has been given.

As I've mentioned, I was often encouraged to "look it up" when I was young. That habit has followed me into adulthood, and sometimes I find myself looking up commonplace words just to see if there's something new to discover in their definition—some deeper clue to notions and concepts we tend to take for granted.

What I learned about the word *deserve* is that it derives from Old French and has been in use in English since the thirteenth century. Its dictionary definition is as follows: "To merit, be qualified for, or have a claim to . . . because of one's acts or qualities."

Aha! Eureka! *Because of one's acts and qualities.*

In other words, deserving is as deserving does. It has nothing to do with circumstances of birth. It has to do with what we make of those circumstances.

When I was young, I sometimes noticed that my

mother would bristle a little when the word *deserve* came up in conversation. I didn't really understand why it irked her; now I think I do. Not only was the word being used imprecisely, it also reflected an unconscious bias: that some people just naturally deserved success or happiness or recognition, and others did not. That idea offended my mother—and it offends me as well.

In my mother's generous view, if *anybody* deserved good fortune, then *everybody* did. And since, in real life, the good luck obviously wasn't shared out equally, then maybe this whole notion of "deserving" was fundamentally flawed.

So I'd like to propose a distinction that, in my mind at least, has become a crucial one: There is a profound difference between *deserving* good fortune and *becoming worthy of* our luck. Deserving is something that happens to us—or maybe simply something we imagine; becoming worthy is something we *do*.

To put it somewhat differently, we can earn our luck *after* we've received it. How? By regarding our good fortune not as an entitlement but as an opportunity to spread the luck around; by seeing our advantages not as a free pass out of hard work and personal challenge, but as a goad to further accomplishment.

Let me suggest an analogy. Like all analogies, this one is imperfect, but I hope that it will resonate and help to clarify what I'm trying to say.

Remember the Calvinist idea of "grace made manifest"? Basically, the concept was that God dispensed a special grace to certain people; but since God's will was unknowable, there was no *direct* way to tell who had this special gift and who did not. Grace, rather, could only be inferred from what a person accomplished in the world. By doing well and doing good, a person demonstrated that he must have had this special grace all along. The logic may have been circular, but in ethical terms the results were all to the good. People behaved honorably and generously as a way of proving they were worthy of the grace they had presumably received.

Now, if we substitute for "God" some more ecumenical notion of the Universe, and if we step away from the tenets of any particular religion, we're getting close to what I mean. Secular advantages such as loving, nurturing parents and economic security are, in fact, a kind of grace—a gift bestowed on us through no merit of our own. But the gift becomes meaningful—becomes truly our own—only by virtue of what we do with it, by how we return it to the world.

What do we make of the head start we've been given? How do we care for and honor the gifts we've received, so that we can pay them back somehow, rather than squander them? How do we show our gratitude?

• • •

• • •

Even though it seems perfectly clear that none of us deserves the particular start we get in life, there will always be certain smug people who imagine that they are somehow entitled to their good fortune. Sometimes these people invoke the Deity in justifying their high station, as if Providence had nothing more important to do than to keep them pampered and insulated. Sometimes they point to heredity—as though a long-ago ancestor who earned a land grant or founded a company has any direct bearing on their own worthiness. Sometimes these smug people seem not even to have given a thought to the whims of fortune that have favored them; the luck of the draw has gone their way, so why question the process?

All of us have probably met people like this at one time or another. They may be the snobs (and sometimes the cheaters) at school; the suave but ineffectual malingerers on the job—people who think they can substitute political savvy for hard work. They tend to be brats on the golf course; in tennis they often feature good form and poor sportsmanship. In friendships, they are sometimes quite entertaining and thoroughly unreliable.

In short, these are people who've been spoiled by advantages they were born to but have not earned.

If we don't look too closely, it is easy to envy these people—if, that is, we ourselves value the things that seem to define them. They tend to have nice manners and nice cars. They have elegant hobbies, like sailing and dressage. Even when they don't seem especially bright or intellectually vibrant, they tend to have credentials from all the right schools, as well as far-flung contacts who can ease their entry into business or a profession. Whereas most folks have to grind their way through life, these people seem to glide. Sure of their prerogatives, blithe in their approach to situations, they seem to cruise along and get what they want.

Enviable, right?

Maybe not so much, if we look a little deeper.

Beneath the well-scrubbed skins and polished manners of many of these privileged people, something seems to be missing. The apparent confidence turns out to be tenuous and brittle—not *true* confidence at all, but simply the habit of *appearing* to be on top of things. The somewhat manic enjoyment of the toys—the cars, the boats, the summer houses—turns out to be imperfect compensation for things that are more precious, subtle, and elusive: a sense of purpose, a knowledge and acceptance of who they really are, a meaningful connection between the things they *have* and the things they yearn for in their hearts.

Most basically of all, the easy charm and the fashionable cynicism often prove to be an elaborate but ultimately ineffective mask for a lack of self-respect. *Self-respect can come only from earning your own reward.* That is absolutely essential. And many of these privileged but empty people—often through no fault of their own—have been deprived of that difficult but redemptive adventure. Their families have handed them luxurious but diminished lives. As my father might put it, they were born with silver daggers in their backs.

No father wants to deprive his son or daughter of the best possible chance of leading a full and satisfying life. No mother wants to hold her child back in the quest for self-respect and personal fulfillment. Why, then, do so many well-meaning families get it wrong?

Part of the reason, I think, is that the particular difficulties and dangers facing well-to-do families just aren't taken seriously enough. Everyone knows that money can't buy happiness; but there's also a widespread if tacit understanding that happiness can't buy money! All in all, it's easier to handle some of life's necessities if one has the money to do so; but that does not justify the leap to believing that money solves all problems or makes one's pain unreal. And let's be honest here: It's also true that, at a time when so many families are struggling to make ends meet, it's a little difficult to drum up sympathy for the children of the wealthy.

That said, it is a fact that the sons and daughters of affluent households face particular challenges and particular pitfalls. These issues are real; they are valid; they may not have to do with the most basic survival needs of a roof over one's head and food on the table, but they are decidedly not trivial.

Many clinical studies support this. I recently came across one by the psychologist Dr. Madeline Levine, author of *The Price of Privilege*. Based on a 2007 study, Dr. Levine concluded that 30 to 40 percent of adolescents from affluent homes experience troubling psychological symptoms. Among teenage girls in this demographic, 22 percent suffer from clinical depression; that's three times the national average. Ten to 15 percent of those who suffer from depression eventually commit suicide.

Clearly, these are serious matters. But even in those instances when the problems don't cross the clinical threshold and the consequences are not so dramatic, the difficulties are often damaging. What are the mistakes that parents make, and that result in inflicting these unintentional hurts upon their kids?

At the most basic level, the errors, I believe, fall into two broad categories. The first is substituting money for love.

Much has been written about this in parenting manuals and magazine articles, so I won't belabor the point here. But I would like to get my two cents in on an aspect of the problem that perhaps goes too little discussed. When affluent parents give too much in terms of money and too little in terms of love, the reason often comes down to simple laziness and self-involvement.

If you have a credit card in your pocket, it's very easy to buy a kid a toy. That will make her happy for a few minutes—and, maybe more important to certain kinds of parents, will keep her occupied, so that they can return to their own preoccupations. It's much more demanding—and of course far more valuable—to take the time to play with the child, to get down on the floor, join in the game, see how the little girl's mind works, and try to help to stoke her imagination. But that takes real involvement, and not just an American Express card.

Similarly, families with money and connections have the luxury of sending their children to the finest schools—but that's a far different thing than actually taking an active interest in their education. What is Johnny learning in that fancy school? Does he need help with his homework? Is the tuition being paid as a gift to *him*—or is it more an attempt on the parents' part to buy their way out of responsibility for their share of the nurturing, the question-answering, the curiosity-expanding?

Kids are hard to fool on matters like this. It occurs to me that they have a certain wisdom that people tend to forget in later life. Kids know that time is more important than money. Grown-ups, especially when they are in mid-career and savoring their prime earning years, tend to act as though the opposite were true. Then, in later life, when money has lost its novelty and time is growing short, they come back to their original understanding. By then, however, their kids are grown, their families are scattered, and the time that wasn't spent together is never coming back.

The tragedy of this was captured beautifully some years ago in a song by Harry Chapin called "Cat's in the Cradle." There's a refrain sung first from the viewpoint of a busy father, and later in the voice of a busy son. "We're gonna have a good time then . . . we're gonna have a good time then." But somehow it just never happens, and then the song is over.

The second kind of mistake often made by affluent parents is even more germane to our discussion here. If life is what we make it, it is essential that we make it *for ourselves.*

This should not mean that we are incapable of accepting help or that we are barred from using our advantages. But there are a lot of fine lines and shades of gray here. When well-meaning families make things too easy for their sons and daughters, they are subverting their chances for self-esteem, depriving them of the hard knocks that build character and the surviving of which leads to a true and durable confidence.

One of my father's often-quoted tenets is that a parent, if he has the means to do so, should give his children "enough to do anything, but not enough to do nothing." In other words, a head start is fine; a free pass is often a crippling disservice. At some point—and the sooner the better—the training wheels have to come off that shiny new bicycle!

Of all the ways in which affluent parents make things too easy for their sons and daughters, perhaps the most widespread is inviting them into the family business, or steering them into a profession in which a forebear has already succeeded. On the face of it, this seems like a kindness. Why not give Junior a position with unassailable job security and a clear path to the top? Why not ease Sis into a legal or medical specialty in which Mom is already an established expert?

If we think about these matters a little more deeply, though, some troubling questions crop up. These seeming kindnesses—who are they really for? Is going into the family business really what's best for the son, or is it meant to flatter the vanity of the father? Is it about the younger man's dreams, or the older man's power and concern for his legacy? And what about turning to professional contacts to ease the way for a daughter who follows in her mother's footsteps? Is the real motivation a desire to help the younger woman, or to swap favors with a powerful colleague and thereby reassert the older woman's own importance?

Where is the line, in other words, between *helping* one's kids and manipulating them so as to perpetuate one's own ambitions and priorities? I raise this question in the full understanding that it can only be answered in the heart and conscience of each individual parent.

For my own parents, the priority was clear. Their hope for my siblings and me was that each of us would find a passion and pursue it with all our diligence and energy—that we should claim our own lives, put our own stamp on everything we did.

But a distinction is in order: This was our parents' *wish* for us, not an expectation. They understood that finding a passion was a difficult and mysterious process, one that required freedom and could only be hampered by family pressure. So we were encouraged to choose for ourselves. Moreover, we absorbed the lesson that what mattered was not the status or monetary potential of our choice, but the honesty and wholeheartedness with which we chose it. If I had decided that my joy in life was picking up trash, my parents would have been fine with seeing me hanging from the back of a truck all day. If I was happy in my calling, that would have sufficed for them.

Was there any pressure to join the family business or to follow the path blazed by my father? Well, my brother, Howie, is a farmer and photographer; my sister, Susie, raised two wonderful children in Omaha; and I found my way into a career in music. So I guess that answers that!

Would my father have helped me get started if I'd chosen a career on Wall Street (which I actually considered for about fifteen minutes)? I'm sure he would have. Would he have given me a job at Berkshire Hathaway if I'd asked for one? I suppose so. But here's the point I'd like to make: In either of those cases, the onus would have been on *me* to demonstrate that I felt a true vocation for those fields, rather than simply taking the course of least resistance. My father would not have served as an enabler of my taking the easy way out. That would not have been an exercise of privilege, but of diminishment.

As I've said, there are certain smug people who seem to take their advantages entirely for granted, who conveniently overlook the fact that, at the start of life, no one deserves anything. These are people who feel entitlement, not gratitude—people who, if they look around at all, see not a world filled with injustice and inequality, but a situation that suits them pretty well.

Such people are only a very tiny subset of those born to privilege. To be that smug, one would have to be entirely devoid both of perception and of conscience—and, fortunately, hardly anyone is like that.

For the overwhelming majority of privileged people, the situation is more complicated and more subtle. They know, at some level, that their good luck is arbitrary and undeserved, that they are among the fortunate ones in an unfair world. Understandably, they want to enjoy the privileges that have fallen their way, but, as people of conscience, they have difficulty doing so. How can they wholeheartedly savor their good fortune when they know that so many others have been deprived of it?

At the same time, there's a certain resentment that comes from feeling constrained in enjoying one's advantages. *Hey, I didn't ask to be born. Is it my fault life's unfair?*

And then there's feeling ashamed about feeling resentful!

It's a tangled web of emotions, and the sum total of it is what is sometimes known as "gift guilt."

Gift guilt is a simmering malaise that can suck the joy out of privileged lives. It's the grim suspicion that one will forever be unworthy, that one will never be able to do enough to justify one's unearned advantages. Gift guilt is a burden and a drain . . . but you know what? It's better to feel it, and to acknowledge feeling it, than to pretend it isn't there.

This is where the smug people secretly suffer. This is why their seeming confidence is often sham and why their blithe behavior often masks emptiness and misery. As Freud and others have pointed out, it's the things we hide from ourselves, the things we bury, that bother us the most, and for the longest time. In denying the responsibilities that are the other side of privilege, the smug people doom themselves to lives of falseness and unease.

On the other hand, if we acknowledge the issue of gift guilt, we can deal with it head-on and find ways to overcome it.

3

The myth of the level playing field

Politicians and business leaders are extremely fond of talking about a "level playing field."

Economic opportunity should be level. Political power should be level. Access to health care should be level, as should chances of fulfillment in the pursuit of happiness. In an ideal world, *everything* should be level.

But we don't live in an ideal world.

Our world is complex and fascinating and beautiful—but ideal it is not. In the world as it actually is, this mythical level playing field can never be more than a hopeful approximation. At best, it is a goal to strive for; at worst, it becomes an empty cliché, like "catch-22" or "perfect storm"—familiar expressions that seem to fit neatly into many conversations without requiring a great deal of thought or any very rigorous definition.

Like the perfect circle—or the perfect *anything*—the level playing field exists only in the realm of thought, of Platonic ideals. Real life just isn't that tidy. In sports there will always be a home team and a visitor, a favorite and an underdog. In business, there will always be people with fancier credentials and better-placed contacts, and those who lack those advantages. In politics, there will always be those with clout and those without. In terms of material comfort, health care, and even life expectancy, a child born in an African village or on an American Indian reservation faces tougher odds than does a kid born in a Connecticut suburb.

None of this is fair or right. All of it should cause unease to people of conscience.

But there's a silver lining here. The recognition that the playing field is not level should motivate us to do all we can to make it *closer* to level; and those efforts toward equality and fairness can, in turn, relieve the corrosive "gift guilt" that we've been talking about.

The moral imperative to acknowledge life's unfairness and to try, in however small and humble a manner, to alleviate it was impressed upon me early, by my mother. She did this—as was her custom—not by lecturing but by showing me the world and letting me draw my own conclusions.

In the same way that my mother felt it was important to expose me to different churches and different kinds of worship, she also thought it was important for me to understand that people were born into lives of differing circumstances and opportunities. She had friends from all walks of life and she would sometimes take me along on her visits to parts of town that were considered "bad" or "poor." What I saw in those neighborhoods were people who clearly had the same blood running through their veins and love in their hearts and dreams in their heads—they had just been born into situations that would probably make it much more difficult to realize their full potential.

While my mother's attention was generally focused on the plight of individuals, my father has always been more of a big-picture kind of person. Through his eyes, I've come to understand that inequality of opportunity is damaging not only to the people who are disadvantaged, but to society at large.

On a trip to China with Bill and Melinda Gates, my father was struck by the untold thousands of people working in factories and fields—people who, because of the particular system they had been born into, would remain in those humble roles for their entire working lives. How many potential entrepreneurs, inventors, and innovators might be buried in those ranks? Or, as my father put it, "How many Bill Gateses might be laboring on that hillside?"

How many potential works of art would never be created, how many scientific breakthroughs never happen, because people of talent and originality were deprived of the chance to make the most of their gifts? Clearly, *all* of us lose out when opportunity is denied.

So, okay, the world is imperfect, the playing field is tilted—what can any of us do about it? How can we help to make the world at least a tiny bit more fair? How can we use our own advantages to make life more equitable for others? And how does this process, in turn, help us to make the most of our own lives?

There are as many answers to these questions as there are people in the world. The answers come in all shapes and sizes. The big answers are called philanthropy. The small answers reside in everyday acts of kindness. But big or small, the *good* answers are based, I think, on a couple of bedrock premises.

The first and most important premise is that people are equal. This may seem obvious; it isn't. Too often, even well-meaning folks confuse people's *circumstances* with their essence. But circumstances vary widely; essences do not. If you believe in the dignity and value of *any* human life—including your own!—then you should recognize the equal dignity and value of *every* human life.

Sadly, seeming acts of kindness are sometimes tainted

by a failure—maybe an unconscious failure—to accept this basic truth. But if people imagine that they are somehow superior to those they are helping, the result is not true kindness, but condescension.

The second premise is more complicated and has to do with a humble acceptance of the limits to how much we can know and how much we can accomplish.

We can only *try* to help others; we can seldom be certain of how much, if at all, we are actually helping. To insist on results, to expect to be thanked—these are not charitable impulses, but selfish ones. That's why the purest donor is the anonymous donor.

Moreover, it is arrogant to imagine that we know what other people need better than they know it themselves. (This, of course, was the central folly of colonizers and missionaries who believed they could "improve" the lives of indigenous peoples by bringing them Western clothes and Western morals and Western religion, trampling on local cultures and traditions in the process.)

As a corollary to this, it is probably a fantasy to think we can say with certainty what constitutes an "advantage" or a "disadvantage." Life is not that simple. We deal in shades of gray.

Let me illustrate this by an example.

A friend of mine, when he was a student at New York University, took a part-time job with Children's Aid Society. This fellow came from a working-class background.

He was getting through school on a mix of scholarships, loans, afternoon jobs, and full-time summer work. Still, he realized that he was more privileged than many people, who wouldn't get to college at all. His relative advantage was not simply economic; it had to do largely with coming from a supportive family that put a high value on education. His family had imbued him with the curiosity to learn, and the confidence that he could do well in a competitive academic setting.

The branch of Children's Aid Society where he worked was in Manhattan's East Village. Far from being the trendy, gentrified neighborhood this area has since become, it was, at the time, a grim precinct of neglected tenements, abandoned cars, and burning mattresses. The area's public schools were subpar, their resources stretched to the breaking point. Among adults and adolescents, heroin use was widespread; burglaries and muggings were everyday occurrences. An intact family household was a rarity. In short, kids who started their lives in these circumstances faced a playing field that was steeply angled against them.

"I had a group of about a dozen boys," my friend recalls, "and when I started working with them, I was completely overwhelmed. I had so little time with them—eight or ten hours a week—and there was so much I hoped to accomplish. I was desperate to understand what they were up against, and so I made what I think is a common mistake: I oversimplified. I imagined that all their difficulties could be explained in terms of poverty. That was what they all had in common, right?

"But as I got to know the kids better, I realized how inadequate that understanding was. Blaming poverty for everything was a sort of do-gooder's shorthand. But it didn't address the differences among the kids. Some clung to me in a way you would expect from much younger children; they tended to be the ones with absent fathers. Some kept their distance and never quite seemed to trust me; they tended to come from households plagued by drug use and violence. Some kids seemed to use our center mainly as a refuge where they could sit quietly with a book. Other kids, whose curiosity had been squelched and whose academic confidence had been damaged, had formed the conviction that books were for sissies. And of course there were the troublemakers—high-energy kids who were always testing the limits, practically daring you to punish them."

Years later, by coincidence, my friend worked for a time as a teacher in a prestigious Manhattan private school.

"And you know what?" he told me. "I saw many of the exact same behaviors and problems I'd seen at Children's Aid."

The school where my friend taught had a particular mandate. It was geared toward "gifted underachievers."

"This was code," he recalled, "for messed-up rich kids. Kids who'd been kicked out of other schools, and whose parents were paying thirty grand a year to buy them one more chance."

What happened to the tilt of the playing field for *those* kids? Economically speaking, the world certainly seemed to be leaning in their favor. Why didn't it seem to be working out that way?

"Rich kids, poor kids," said my friend. "I stopped seeing the divide and started seeing the universal. The parents of the kids at the fancy school tended to be obsessed with their own careers and social lives; a few were even celebrities. Their kids were a lot like the fatherless ones from Children's Aid—tender, clingy, always needing more attention and reassurance. The ones whose parents were abusive or belittling tended to be angry and mistrustful toward me before I'd ever said a word. And of course we had the limit-testers—kids who were always flirting with expulsion, which would make Mom and Dad have to deal with them again."

What did my friend learn from his experiences with kids from these different ends of the economic spectrum? One lesson, clearly, was that if we equate the word *privileged* simply with the idea of *having money,* we're painting over a lot of gray areas and overlooking a lot of other factors. Good parenting, it seemed, could conquer at least some of the difficulties that attached to being poor. Bad parenting could easily squander the supposed advantages that accrued to affluence. You could not categorically say that one group of kids was happier, or better adjusted, or more prepared to make the most of their own lives, than the other.

My friend took away some more personal lessons as well. "In both situations," he told me, "I went in wanting to help, and in both cases it turned out I had far more to learn than to teach.

"From the poor kids, I learned a lot about the mystery of identity—this really humbling and inspiring strength of character that allows certain people to remain undaunted in any situation. Where does that courage come from? How did these kids hang on to their optimism? As for the rest of us—weren't we wimps if we gave in to discouragement?

"From the rich kids," he went on, "I learned a different lesson—something about myself. When I started that job, I had a chip on my shoulder, a class resentment. *My* parents couldn't have shelled out thirty grand for private school; why did *these* kids get to go? As I got to know them as people, though—as I saw their vulnerabilities and sensed their pain—I realized that I had to let go of that attitude. Compassion wasn't true compassion if it only applied to people who had less than you; compassion should apply to everyone who could use a little help and understanding—which is to say, everyone in the world."

My friend mentioned one final thing he'd learned from these experiences—maybe the most pertinent of all to our discussion. He came away with a better perspective and a greater acceptance of the tilt of his *own* particular playing field. "I realized," he said, "that no two people have exactly the same mix of advantages and disadvantages, and besides, it all depends what you make of it. Shift your course a little, and a headwind becomes a tailwind. Keep plugging, and eventually the sun that's in your eyes will be at your back. It doesn't matter so much where you start in life; it matters where you go."

Given that a truly, perfectly level playing field is an impossible ideal, and considering that no two people have precisely the same contours in their personal landscapes, does a favorable tilt necessarily call into question or diminish the value of what one accomplishes?

This, I believe, is a serious and even tormenting question to many people of privileged backgrounds. Can they truly believe that their achievements are their own? Is their self-respect compromised by the knowledge that they had a head start or a crucial boost somewhere along the line? How can they attain the satisfaction of knowing that they earned their own reward?

In fields where a person's performance is measurable and public, these questions are easy to answer. Consider an example from the world of sports.

Ken Griffey Jr. is the son of a very fine major-league

baseball player and he had all sorts of advantages in starting his own career. From an early age, he learned skills from his dad; he absorbed the professional athlete's ethos from hanging around clubhouses and dugouts. Coaches and scouts kept a special eye on him. But so what? Can anyone doubt that when Ken Griffey Jr. hits a home run, it's *his* home run? Clearly, the background ceases to matter when he steps out onto the field, alone, and is defined by his own performance. When Junior is inevitably inducted into the Hall of Fame, it will be his own excellence and determination that got him there.

Or again, consider a case from the entertainment field. Kate Hudson is the daughter of Goldie Hawn. Besides inheriting a lovely face, she grew up in a Hollywood milieu, with special access to agents, producers, and directors. But again, so what? When she interprets a role or steps in front of a camera, these advantages fade into deep background. All that matters is the commitment and talent that she herself brings to the moment.

It's also worth noting that all the head starts and connections in the world are not enough to ensure success if talent and passion are lacking. Remember Nancy Sinatra and Frank Sinatra Jr.? Clearly, every door was open to them, and their musical ability just didn't measure up to the standard set by their famous father. I do not say this disparagingly; the Sinatra kids took their shot, and good for them. My point is that in fields where success and failure, excellence and mediocrity, are measurable and public, it's relatively easy to see the line between inherited advantages and personal accomplishments.

Most of us, however, don't operate in fields that are so neatly defined by batting averages or Oscar nominations or Grammys—and that's where it gets tricky. Most of us have to decide for ourselves—in our secret hearts and most honest thoughts—if we are truly earning our own reward or just cruising on unearned momentum. But what are the criteria by which we can judge?

For starters, I think a simple but crucial gut-test is in order. When we are choosing a career or life path, I think we need to ask ourselves if we are making that choice out of true conviction, or because it's where our advantages lie. To put it another way, are we really choosing the "game" we want to play, or are we abdicating that choice and just letting the slope of the playing field make our decision for us?

As I've mentioned, I briefly considered a career on Wall Street. Would I have enjoyed this? Probably not. Would I have been any good at it? We'll never know. For sure, though, I would have benefited from a very favorable tilt if I'd entered that profession. Someone would have hired me, if only as a favor to my father. Chances are I would have been especially looked out for and groomed to advance. I would have been hard to fire!

Now, if I'd felt a passion for banking or investing, if I

really had believed that a career on Wall Street was what I was put on Earth to do, I probably would have gone for it *in spite of* my advantages. Let people say he only made it because he's Warren Buffett's son! Why would I have cared? I'd have found a way to make my accomplishments my own . . . *if* I had felt a true commitment to what I was doing.

But that *if* is all-important. It's the thing that dooms or redeems us.

In my own case, I ran a gut-check and concluded pretty readily that Wall Street was not for me. As a career move, I suppose it would have been a savvy choice, but in a deeper way it would have felt like a surrender, a failure of imagination.

That gut-check was nobody's business but my own; no one else could have run it for me. No one else can run *yours* either. Each of us must decide for himself or herself where the passion is—even if it steers us to a part of the playing field where the tilt is steeply upward.

4

The (mixed) blessing of choice

When I was a teenager, I'd already had long exposure to a remarkable work ethic—my father's. I'd also drawn many lessons from what I think of as my mother's humanitarian ethic—her boundless curiosity about all sorts of people and her undaunted determination to connect with them, to hear their stories and understand their lives.

But for all of that, when it came to my own future and the decisions that would shape it, I was as vague, confused, and uncommitted as many if not most teenagers.

I wasn't even sure I wanted to finish high school—or not in the usual way at least. Eager to get on with my life, I thought about going for early graduation and skipping senior year.

I'd taken a keen interest in photography—an interest that began with a Boys Club course way back in eighth grade. I wasn't very interested in sports; music was a hobby but not yet a passion. I needed another activity in my life—something I could be good at, and that, in turn, would help define who I was. Photography filled the bill. By the time I was in high school, I was regularly submitting pictures to the school paper and the yearbook; I'd also taken a summer job on the local weekly newspaper. I was learning more every day, and the camera had become an important part of my identity.

With this modest success as background, I'd formed a rather romantic if less than fully baked plan. I wanted to finish high school early, then move to Jackson Hole, Wyoming, where I would support myself as a photojournalist while enjoying the great outdoors amid some of the most magnificent scenery on Earth.

As youthful schemes go, this one was not entirely farfetched. I *did* have some published pictures to my credit. I *might* have gotten a newspaper job and started a career in Jackson Hole. We'll never know—because my parents had quite different ideas about what I ought to be doing at that stage of my life. Their sober and reasonable expectations trumped my adolescent fantasies.

And this brings us to some very complicated areas. It raises difficult questions—questions that probably don't have definitive answers, since every family is different.

For example: Where's the line between loving parental guidance, and too much interference? At what point does *help* become *control*? How much parenting is too much parenting, and how does that change as a child grows up? How much choice does a young person really have in choosing his or her own path? How much latitude *should* that person have? Is there such a thing as too much freedom, too many choices?

In the Buffett household, there was a fundamental paradox in these matters. It was not my parents' style to tell us kids what we should do or what we should be. On the contrary, the constant lesson of our upbringing was that we could be whatever we wanted to be, that we should follow our hearts wherever they led us.

But life is never quite that simple, is it?

Because parallel to the *explicit* message that our choices were our own to make and that our freedom was essentially limitless was a pattern of *implicit* messages that tended to guide the choices and circumscribe the freedom. These implicit messages, of course, took the form of parental expectations. Every family has them. They seldom need to be spoken aloud.

One of the tacit expectations in our family was that the kids would do their best in school. I wasn't pressured to get straight A's, but it was assumed that I would take school seriously and apply myself. This assumption was by no means a bad thing. It set in motion a positive dynamic:

I'm expected to do well in school; that must mean I *can* do well in school; armed with that confidence, I do well in school and feel good about it.

But this brings me back to my youthful plan to skip senior year and get out into the world. At this juncture the explicit message—*Find your bliss!*—collided head-on with the implicit message—*Don't find your bliss too soon . . . and don't skip steps along the way.*

As a typically impatient young man, I couldn't help seeing this second message simply as an unwanted brake on my enthusiasm, a way to thwart my freedom. Later in life, however, I came to realize that the admonition contained a valuable lesson whose nuances I hadn't previously grasped. My parents weren't trying to hold me back. Rather, they were counseling me not to move too fast through the processes of growing up, out of a concern that I might, in my hurry, miss something wonderful. My adult life was out there in the future, waiting for me to show up and inhabit it. Reaching it would probably entail a sometimes stumbling journey, but I might lose more than I would gain by taking shortcuts.

In any case, my intention to leave school caused my parents a fair bit of consternation, and finally, near the end of my junior year, my mother intervened. Fortunately, I didn't learn of this until later; if I had known about it at the time, I might have been launched into a phase of adolescent rebellion that would have strained family relationships and possibly shortchanged my own future.

Here's what happened:

One day, in the spring of junior year, my journalism teacher asked to have a private word with me. He let me know that he intended to give me the job of yearbook editor in my senior year—*if*, of course, I would reconsider my plan to graduate early. It was an honor to be asked; the editorship would give me a structured way to continue with my photography. I don't think I hesitated in accepting. (This no doubt says something about the level of my commitment to Jackson Hole—but that's adolescence for you!)

Sometime late in my senior year, I learned that the previous spring my mother had approached my journalism teacher, and the two of them had hatched this plan together.

How did I feel about this? Well, the fact that I'm still thinking about it thirty-five years later should give you some idea of the complexity of my emotions.

On the one hand, I know now, and *sort of* knew even then, that my mother was right in lobbying to have me stay in school. And I do believe that my journalism teacher sincerely wanted me as editor.

But still . . . two adults, without my knowledge, had conspired to shift my path. This was disconcerting. I wasn't sure if I should appreciate the intervention, or resent it.

At some level I probably did both. I never doubted that the grown-ups had my best interests at heart; but even so, their involvement made me uneasy and raised some uncomfortable but inevitable doubts in my mind. The editorship was a modest enough accomplishment . . . but could I really be sure it was my own? Was I being gently guided toward my own proper destiny, or was I—again, with the best possible intentions—being subverted in my quest to become my own person and claim my own life?

If anyone is expecting a tidy or definitive conclusion to this anecdote, I must apologize; I don't have one. The story raises questions that have no easy answers. About all that can be said with certainty is this: It's hard to be a parent and it's hard to be a kid, and there's no such thing as being perfect in either role. (In fact, it's probably when people *try* to be perfect that things like hypocrisy and nervous breakdowns happen!) Loving moms and dads will always feel an impulse to insert themselves into a kid's development; sometimes, inevitably, they will overstep. Kids will always chafe at what feels like grown-up meddling—even when they themselves are heading for a bad decision. That's life.

But it occurs to me that what matters about these inevitable parent-child controversies is not the clash of wills that causes them, but the decisions and new understandings that come out of them. I'll never know how my life would have turned out if I'd taken off for Jackson Hole. But I *do* know that staying home and finishing school turned out to be the right decision. I'd wanted to believe that I was ready and able to face the world alone; I now accept the reality that I probably was not. I was *in the process* of learning to make good decisions and enjoy the luxury of freedom, but I wasn't quite there yet. There was something almost Zen about how it all turned out: I found my path not by exercising my will but by yielding it.

And by the way, I'm very proud of the yearbook we produced my senior year.

This story about the yearbook brings me to a more general topic—again, a subject that contains a lot of gray areas, ambivalence, and possible discomfort. It's about the effect on kids when parents pull strings to get them special treatment or particular advantages.

As I've said, my family was not rich when I was growing up. By the time I was an adolescent, though, my father had come to be fairly well known and very respected; he had powerful friends and access to almost everyone. And there is no getting around the fact that the Buffett name—plus a recommendation letter from Katharine Graham, the publisher of *The Washington Post*—helped get me into Stanford.

There is nothing terribly unusual about this. All private universities offer a certain number of "legacy" admissions to the offspring of illustrious alumni and prospective donors, and these kids generally mix in well enough with the ones who got in by way of double-800s and valedictorian speeches. Is the system fair? Not really. But "the system" is not what concerns me here. Rather, it's the system's effect on individuals.

To be honest, I'm not exactly sure why I agreed to go to Stanford. Was I, at that stage of my life, burning with enthusiasm for higher education? I can't say that I was. Did I feel a great affinity for that school in particular? I can't say that I did. The truth—as well as I can pin it down—is that I went to Stanford because I knew it was a privilege to go to Stanford. It was an opportunity I felt I should not pass up, rather than an adventure I longed to claim as my own.

In brief, my motivation was rather circular and lukewarm, long on obligation but short on joy; no doubt that's part of the reason I left school after three semesters. I'll have more to say about this decision in due course; but for now I just want to mention one more possible factor in my choosing to leave: I'm not sure I ever really believed that I *deserved* to be at Stanford in the first place.

Would I have been accepted if I had a different last name? Would my application have impressed without the A-list recommendations? Was I as worthy of my privileged seat in the classroom as the kid with the four-point-oh average all through school and the perfect SATs?

I can't say I lay awake nights worrying about these questions, but still, in some measure they undermined my confidence and compromised my legitimacy in the only place it really matters: *in my own mind.*

Was my father wrong in helping me get into Stanford? Of course not. What parent doesn't want to help his child advance in life? But I think this is another of those dilemmas without a clear solution; another illustration of the impossibility of being a perfect parent or an adolescent without issues.

Humility is called for here; parents generally know more than kids do, but no one really knows enough. We proceed with good intentions and hope that our true motives are pure. Sometimes—let's face it—those motives are more complex than people like to admit. We've probably all known families who send their sons and daughters to Harvard or Yale so they can boast that they have a kid at Harvard or Yale. *Oh. Your kid's bumming around Europe for a year? My kid's pre-law at Princeton.* Can we say for sure which young person is having the more valuable experience? And is the Princeton tuition paying primarily for the kid's education or the parents' vanity?

There are as many answers as families. And I'm not trying to make trouble! Just raising the question.

For as long as I remained at Stanford, I tried to make the most of it, and my lack of clear direction turned out, in a way, to be a blessing. If I wasn't passionately interested in anything in particular, I was at least mildly curious about *everything.* So I signed on for as many courses as I could carry, as long as they ended in "101" or "ology."

Call me a dilettante—but only if you keep in mind the origin of the word. It derives from the Italian verb *dilettare,* which means "to take delight." And that's exactly what I was doing—taking delight in the amazing variety and richness of a liberal education. This was the real privilege of being at a school like Stanford, though I probably didn't appreciate it fully at the time. I could read the great philosophers, study the basic sciences, dabble in literature—without the immediate pressure of choosing a major whose demands would narrow my focus, and that would funnel me toward a career whose rigors and competitiveness would limit my choices still further.

The setting of a liberal arts college nurtured my far-flung curiosity; but I now understand that my sense of freedom, of having options, had been fostered much earlier, by my family. Of all the gifts my parents gave me, this was surely among the most valuable: the belief that I need not be squeezed by life, that I could take an expansive view of how I wanted to spend my time on Earth rather than shrinking myself down to fit into some predetermined niche.

During my freshman year at Stanford, there was an incident that really made me understand what a rare and precious gift this freedom was.

I was walking down the hallway of my dorm one day, when I heard a young woman, an acquaintance, in the midst of an emotional conversation on the telephone. (Yes, strange but true, once upon a time there were no cell phones, and college kids called home, usually collect, from pay phones in the hall!) Not wanting to eavesdrop or intrude, I moved discreetly away. A few moments later, my schoolmate came down the hallway crying.

I asked her what was wrong. It turned out that she was crying tears of joy and relief. She'd just spoken to her father. She'd poured out her heart to him, told him how unhappy she was, how overwhelmed. How, if she continued on her present course, she saw nothing but misery in her future, maybe even failure. Her father heard her out, then finally said, okay, she didn't have to be a doctor. She could be a lawyer.

My schoolmate, wiping away tears and almost laughing now from the release of all that pressure, said, "Isn't it wonderful?"

I stood there, fumbling for something helpful and supportive to say, but all I could think of was *Nice that you have a choice . . . but that's* it*?! Doctor or lawyer? Of all the possible things you could be, you're supposed to pick between two?*

I don't remember what I actually said. Maybe I just nodded. But the incident started me thinking about a number of things. One of them, of course, was about options and how different people choose among them. Another line of thought was about the complex and sometimes paradoxical relationship between choices and privilege.

If we think about it, what does *privilege* really mean? Too often, I believe, people think of privilege only in terms of money and the things that money can buy. To be privileged is to live in a comfortable home, have enough good food to eat, wear nice clothes, sleep in a clean bed that is cool enough in summer and warm enough in winter. And all of that is fine, as far as it goes. But is it the *essence* of what it means to be privileged? I think not.

If life is what we make it, if we ourselves take up the challenge of creating the lives we want, then it seems clear to me that the essence of privilege has to do with having the widest possible array of options.

Think about all the many people who—by our conventional measures, at least—are *not* privileged. The African villager who, because of a corrupt government or a lack of educational opportunities, can only remain a bare subsistence farmer or the tender of a few meager cattle. The inner-city youth or an American Indian on an impoverished reservation, whose horizons are cut short by a culture of broken families and despair. Or, for that matter, those Chinese workers whose society keeps them in the factories or on the farms where they happened to start. For people in these circumstances, survival tends to be a full-time job. Food and shelter for themselves and their families must obviously come first. But economic security and material comfort are not the only things these people are deprived of; they're often deprived of *choice*. And, if you think about it, a lack of options is every bit as cruel as any other lack. Hunger and thirst can be satisfied from day to day. But a frustrated yearning for change, for new possibilities, can last a lifetime—or even be passed down through generations.

Which brings me back to my schoolmate at Stanford. Clearly, she was "privileged." Her family was well-to-do; she had the opportunity of a world-class education. In theory, her options were virtually boundless.

In practice, though, her possibilities were being squeezed by her family's biases about what constituted a "good" or an "appropriate" or a "socially acceptable" career choice. Not that there's anything wrong, of course, with becoming a doctor or a lawyer, if that's truly what one *wants* to be. But that's exactly the point I'm getting at. In the case of my schoolmate, what *she wanted* didn't seem to count for much in the equation. Her future was being imposed on her—and, as of that time at least, she was allowing it to happen.

In other words, she was privileged, and yet she viewed her range of options as if she wasn't. How perverse is that? With one hand, her parents had given her a universe of possibilities; with the other hand, they were taking most of them away. What if she wanted to be a teacher, say, or a dancer? What if she wanted to do any of the myriad things that would lead to a less secure livelihood, but perhaps greater satisfaction? What if her true leaning was toward a career that—in our particular culture at that particular moment—was less prestigious?

No doubt, this young woman's family had her best interests at heart—or thought they did. They wanted her to have a life of material comfort and social status. They wanted her to make the *right* choice.

But the right choice isn't necessarily the safe or comfortable or obvious choice. It usually isn't the choice that's made for us by someone else. And if it's a choice that must be made between rigid and narrow alternatives, that's a waste of what we think of as privilege.

As a sort of counterpoint to this anecdote about my Stanford schoolmate, let me tell you a happier story.

There's a saying—I've seen it on bumper stickers and T-shirts, though I wouldn't be at all surprised if it derived from Buddha or Lao Tse—that goes "Not all who wander are lost." I happen to believe there's a kernel of deep truth in this statement—even though it can easily be taken too far. I mean, some who wander *are* lost, and that's just how it is! But there are many circumstances in which wandering through a labyrinth of choices is not a symptom of being lost, but a necessary passage on the road to being found.

A friend recently told me about a former schoolmate of his, who changed majors practically every semester. He started college intending to become a mechanical engineer. But he soon grew bored with the concrete, hands-on aspect of engineering; he had a hankering for something more ethereal and abstract.

So he changed his major to physics. This captivated him for a while, but he found that what he really loved about the subject was the beautiful and orderly patterns it described.

So he switched his major to math, which was about nothing *but* patterns, completely divorced from physical objects. Math held his interest for a semester or two, until he began to feel that his world was becoming *too* abstract. His mind now yearned for things he could see with his eyes and touch with his hands.

He changed majors again, and this time he changed colleges, too. By now, his parents were no doubt pulling their hair out, and even his friends were wondering if he was simply one of those people who was very bright and incurably flaky. He enrolled at the Rhode Island School of Design as a fine arts major, with a concentration on drawing and painting.

The leap was not as off-the-wall as it might at first

seem. This fellow was obsessed with beautiful patterns. But the splendid patterns of mathematics were invisible, and he longed to bring them into the light of day somehow. So why not try to render something analogous to them in a beautifully wrought line or composition or mix of colors?

But—surprise!—the painting option didn't quite work out for this fellow. First of all, he had some doubts as to whether he was talented enough, whether he could translate his intellectual ideas about painting into actual artworks. And aside from that, he found the painter's life too solitary, too removed from the common experiences and conduct of business that connect most people.

So he changed majors yet again, this time to architecture. Architecture was collaborative and social; it was both an art and a business. Design called for a knowledge of physics and of mathematical relationships. It allowed him to use his drawing skills and to exercise his love of patterns. He'd finally found his calling, right?

Well, almost. There were a couple things about architecture that still frustrated him. One was that most designs for buildings never got built; they lived and died as blueprints. What about the steel and glass and stone they were envisioned to be built from? This fellow found himself getting more and more interested in *materials* and their different characteristics. In other words, he'd come full circle and was thinking like a mechanical engineer!

And these hypothetical buildings—how would they fit in the pattern of a city, among its grids and contours? How would their esthetics and their scale and the nature and cost of their materials affect the people who lived and worked in them? What was the *larger* pattern these buildings would inhabit?

Eureka! He finally had it—the discipline that matched his broadest interests and employed his fullest skill set. He was meant to be an urban planner. He changed his major one last time, worked through to a master's degree, and went on to a distinguished and satisfying career.

So—was this fellow "lost" during the years of his academic wanderings? Or was he following a path that was not yet visible but was nonetheless taking him where he was meant to go?

Is there such a thing as too much freedom or having too many choices?

I believe the answer is no, though it's easy to see why some people view it otherwise. There are many instances of young people making bad, destructive use of the freedom they have, or of being overwhelmed by the options with which life has presented them. When kids get into trouble with drugs, that's obviously a disastrous misuse of their freedom, though not a *result* of their freedom; very often the drug use is symptomatic of other issues for which the user has yet to find better, healthier solutions. When young people blunder into adulthood without ambition or direction, chances are it has to do with an inability to choose a path and forswear other possibilities.

But let's be clear and let's not make excuses. When people make bad use of their freedom, it isn't freedom's fault; it's their fault!

Freedom must be managed. It must be tempered from within. My mother had a saying—practically a mantra—that sums this up. She used to tell me that I could be whatever I wanted to be, but not do whatever I wanted to do. In other words, my aspirations could be boundless, but my *behavior* was subject to right and fitting limits. These limits were defined by personal morality and integrity, and by commonly shared ideas of decency and ethics. These things were not intended to crimp my freedom, but rather to give it direction and shape. Freedom, after all, is different from anarchy, lawlessness, or chaos!

Similarly, when people get tangled up in their options, it's not because they have too many; it's because they lack the clarity and will to commit to one.

But how does a person achieve that clarity and develop that commitment? This brings us to the complicated subject of vocation.

5

The mystery of vocation

In the autumn of 2008, I had the honor of performing at both the New York and Los Angeles branches of the Paley Center for Media. This opportunity was very meaningful to me, for at least a couple reasons. The performances—a mix of music, video footage, and conversation—gave me a chance to share and refine many of the thoughts that, in turn, have shaped this book. And the Los Angeles concert was very special for me because my father was able to attend.

It was the first time he'd ever heard me play and sing in such a public setting. But he didn't just listen; he joined in. He brought along his somewhat famous ukulele, and we opened the program by doing a song together. After a rousing rendition of "Ain't She Sweet," my father got a good laugh by telling the audience that he was there "to see what I got for my investment in piano lessons."

If I'd thought of it at the time, I might have asked him *which* piano lessons—because I started studying piano, and quit, on four different occasions!

And I think that suggests one of the central points I hope to make here: that life vocations are mysterious, and people seldom move toward them in a straight line, or without doubts and false starts and crises and blunders.

In retrospect, it seems abundantly clear that music was always my calling—which makes it even more of a head-scratcher as to why it took me so long to fully embrace it. In this, I suspect I'm like a lot of people. The things that loom largest, and right in front of our noses, are sometimes the hardest to see.

My mother used to tell me that I toddled around singing "Twinkle, Twinkle, Little Star" before I even learned to talk. From earliest childhood on, I heard tunes in my head—and of course I had no way of knowing that this was the slightest bit unusual. Didn't everybody hear this inner music? As soon as I could reach the piano keys, I pounded on the bass notes to simulate thunder and tickled the high notes to sound like rain.

Here was my idea of a "date" when I was four. I invited a friend named Diana over to my house. She was the first girl I ever had a crush on. I emerged from our fireplace—

which framed me like a proscenium arch—and serenaded her with a Paul Anka song. *Oh, please, stay by me, Di-ana!*

Then, when I was five, an earth-shaking event took place: The Beatles made their first appearance on *The Ed Sullivan Show.* I was smitten; I was overwhelmed. Like millions of other families, the Buffetts ran right out to the local department store and bought a precious piece of vinyl—*Introducing the Beatles,* on Vee-Jay records. I was soon an accomplished—no, relentless—practitioner of air guitar. I imitated John Lennon's knee bend and Paul McCartney's craning of the neck when he sang out his signature *Yeah, yeah, yeah, YEAH!* I spent dozens if not hundreds of hours with this one album, listening on our Sears portable record player. One day the needle broke; I replaced it with one of my mom's sewing needles. It worked! My first foray into the marriage of music and technology.

By the time I was six, I'd started piano lessons. My teacher was the classic "old lady down the street," who taught my older sister as well as other kids in the neighborhood. From her I learned the basics of fingering and harmonies and simple chords and sight reading.

I also learned the difference between a major and a minor key—the first sounds happy and bright, the second dark and sad. This very basic understanding led to a powerful breakthrough about how music could convey emotion, how expressive it could be. One evening—I was probably seven—I was feeling out of sorts. I went over to the piano, which was very near the chair my father always sat in to read the evening paper. Rather than try to explain my funky mood in words, I slowly tapped out "Yankee Doodle" in a minor key. Magically, the sprightly march became a dirge—and my family instantly knew how I was feeling.

But, as much as I loved the piano, and as important as music already was in my life, after two years I wanted to quit my lessons.

Why? This question requires that I interrupt my nostalgic account to consider some issues of more general interest. Why is it so difficult for young people to recognize—and commit to—their true vocation? What are some of the stumbling blocks and probably inevitable passages along the way?

One difficulty, I think, is simply that acknowledging and embracing a calling really raises the stakes in life. Consider: Most people are so-so at most things; that fact is the basis for the whole idea of what's *average*. Nothing wrong with that. Most people are average students, average golfers, average whatever. Garrison Keillor notwithstanding, you can't have a town where everyone's *above* average, because the average would move to keep up!

In most spheres of life, average is plenty good enough.

In fact, there are real advantages to being average. It keeps the pressure off and the expectations manageable.

In terms of one's true vocation, however, being average doesn't cut it. If your calling is to be a chef, being average in the kitchen clearly isn't good enough. No committed teacher wants to be average in the classroom. No author wants to be average on the page.

Our vocations are the fields in which we yearn to excel, to break out of the pack. This yearning is wonderful; it exalts us. It brings out the best in us, and leads us to discoveries and achievements that we can truly claim as our own.

It also explains why embracing a vocation is so scary.

If, in the many facets of life at which we are destined to be average, we come up a little short, so what? But if we fail at the thing by which we define ourselves and at which we hope to prove special, that's serious.

Which brings me back to the first time I quit piano lessons. I was eight years old, and I won't pretend that I was thinking like a grown-up. Insofar as I could articulate my reason for wanting to quit, it was simply that lessons were no longer fun.

But why weren't they?

The answer, I think, is that they were no longer fun because they were becoming difficult; and they were becoming difficult because I was starting to go more deeply into a subject that really mattered to me—something I really wanted to be good at. In however childish a way, I was starting to understand that my relationship to the piano was not a casual one, not something to be taken lightly.

My budding passion for music, therefore, was a source of both joy and a certain discomfort, a certain vague fear.

And I have to believe that this mix of emotions has been experienced by many other people in the early stages of their approach-avoidance dance with their life's calling.

Life is complicated, and, not infrequently, we harbor feelings that at first glance seem to be mutually exclusive but turn out to be entirely compatible. So let me mention one other—paradoxical—component of my decision to quit piano lessons at the ripe old age of eight. At the same time as I was resisting the lessons because of their increasing difficulty, I was developing a confident—if misguided—belief that I could learn music just fine on my own.

What was the point of learning other people's music, written on a page in black and white, when my own simple compositions emerged from some mysterious place in vivid, living color?

If this confidence was bracing, it was also dangerous. It was nice to believe that I had some measure, at least, of originality, some way to make music that was truly my own. But I didn't yet know enough—I wasn't even close—

to bring that ability to fruition, and it would have been self-defeating to imagine that I did. There's a lesson here, I think, for precocious kids who feel the first itch of creativity, and who wrongly imagine that they know more than their teachers.

I had to realize—eventually!—that there are no shortcuts to craft. I had to learn to let myself be taught.

All the great spiritual and religious traditions revere their teachers, and it's interesting that many seem to share the idea that life offers a *multiplicity* of teachers. Buddhism has the maxim "many paths, many guides." Christianity presents us with not one Gospel writer, but four. One of the most important prayers in the Hebrew canon, the Kaddish, was originally a song of praise to a beloved teacher; it evolved into a universal prayer for the dead—the implication being that *everyone* who has gone before us is our teacher.

To put it another way, there are as many teachers as there are things to be learned, and the number is virtually limitless.

I mention this in regard to my piano lessons because I would have three more teachers before I was finished (three *paid* teachers, that is; I would have dozens more who taught or influenced me without ever knowing it or being thanked) and each one would bring something unique and irreplaceable to my rather sporadic education. Good teachers, in any field, do far more than convey information; they pass along something of themselves. So the technical progress that each teacher helped me with was probably less important than the different *approach* that each teacher took.

My first teacher taught piano by the book. Read the notes, count the beats. Put the proper fingers on the proper keys. This was not especially creative, but it was completely appropriate and totally necessary, and it hints at a truth that probably applies in every discipline. You've got to put in some grunt work and master the basics before you can let your imagination soar. Creativity without a foundation in boring old craft leads to more messes than masterpieces.

My second teacher, with whom I started studying in fifth grade, took a subtly but crucially different tack. She was less interested in the notes than in the *sound*. Why did, say, a Simon and Garfunkel song sound different from a Mozart sonata? How many ways could a simple C major chord be voiced? How was it possible that the same instrument could be made to sound like Chopin or Jerry Lee Lewis?

From this second teacher, I learned that every time I put a finger on a key, I was making a choice. Not only what note to play, but how to play it—how to make it sound appropriate to the material I was playing, and, ultimately, how to make it sound like *me*.

My third teacher built on this, and in fact took it to a whole different level. For her, the notes and the rules were only the most basic raw material, meant to be learned so that they could then be transcended. As for the sound, that was only a means to a far more important end: self-expression.

Now the mix was really getting rich! Exciting and terrifying! How did you harness the emotion in your heart, pump it through the knowledge in your brain, and transform it into notes played by your fingers? How much soul and risk-taking and self-exposure went into that equation? How much self-knowledge was required, how much self-abandon? What if you reached deep, put your rawest and most personal feelings into the music, and came up with . . . nothing much?

I wasn't yet ready to chance it. I didn't yet know enough of life or my own heart. I chose to get more involved with the safer and less personal craft of photography. I let my involvement with music slip toward the sidelines one more time.

But enough about me—at least for the moment!

Let's talk a bit more generally about this mysterious subject of vocations, and address some fundamental questions.

First of all, where do these powerful life-callings come

from? I have a simple if unsatisfying answer to that one: no one knows. Obviously, when a child follows in a parent's footsteps, it's tempting to conclude that heredity and/or a deeply ingrained family culture are the determining factors. But what about all those many instances when a young person zigs off in an entirely different direction? The very fine poet James Merrill happened to be a scion of the family that founded Merrill Lynch. How do you explain *his* vocation? The answer is you don't. Rather than explaining it, we can celebrate it as an example of the wonderful complexity of human nature, and of the giddy range of choices that life affords.

The second question I'd like to raise is trickier. Does each and every one of us *have* a life-vocation?

Well, that depends on how we define it. If we take *vocation* to mean a passion for the work we do, then the honest answer is no. In an ideal world, all of us would find our bliss in the same place that we find our paycheck. That would be Utopia! In the real world, it doesn't always work that way. We can strive to succeed in our work; we can strive to excel at our work; unfortunately, that's not the same thing as loving our work, or finding in it the truest expression of who we are.

But I'd like to propose a broader definition of *vocation*—one that potentially includes us all. I'd like to define *vocation* as the tug we feel toward the life that is right for us, the life that is truly our own. That life *might* be centered around work or a particular career; but it doesn't have to be. The bliss of it—the *rightness* of it—can reside in any aspect of a chosen path.

Let me tell you about a couple whose different approaches to life illustrate the range of possibilities I'm trying to explain.

One member of this partnership is a man who knew from childhood on that he was destined to be a writer. "It wasn't necessarily a matter of talent," he says, "but of temperament. I got along okay with other kids, but when I was really concentrating, really focused on something, I wanted to be alone. It was important to me to be able to explain things to myself, to get at the *why* of things. And I discovered early on that I had great discipline—as long as it was *self*-discipline; but if anyone else tried to tell me what to do, I tended to be stubborn, surly, and rebellious. So I wouldn't do too well having a boss—and I guess that disqualified me for ninety-five percent or so of possible careers."

This last comment suggests one of the useful things about a definite work-vocation: It simplifies the landscape by making it very clear what we *don't* want to do!

In any case, this fellow was determined to be a writer, and, he adds, "I never really had a Plan B. I had maybe two moments in my life when I wavered. One was when I started college. Actually making a living as a writer seemed awfully dicey, so I was supposedly a premed student. That lasted until the first biology lab, when I had to pith a frog. I'll spare you the details, but I realized I was way too squeamish to be a doctor. The second spasm of practicality came right after college. I got a job as a pollster during a presidential campaign. This was actually pretty interesting. It gave me the chance to talk with lots of people. But *why* did I want to talk with lots of people? Because it would give me stuff to write about. That was always the central thing."

So this fellow decided that, however dicey it might be, he was going to stake his economic future on his writing. "It's a lucky thing I went for it then," he says, "when I was still young and resilient in the face of all the inevitable rejection. I had basically no money. I lived like a student till I was thirty or so. But I didn't mind. I was doing what I wanted to do. I'm not sure it's even accurate to say it was a choice. I just couldn't imagine doing anything else."

In short, this fellow has led a life that is clearly centered around a work-vocation.

His partner, by contrast, operates in accordance with a calling that could hardly be more different—but that, in my view at least, is just as valid.

"I've never had a capital-C career," this man says, "and never wanted one. I've had plenty of jobs. I accept the necessity of making money. But that's just it—I see it as a necessity. It isn't bad, it isn't good. It's just something you have to do to support your life."

Just as his partner knew early on that he was meant to be a writer, this man understood from a young age that his truest self was not the self that would go off to a job. "In grade school," he recalls, "the teacher would ask the standard question: What do you want to be when you grow up? Kids would say fireman, astronaut, scientist. I'd say *happy*. Some kids would tell me that wasn't a job. And I remember thinking *oh yes it is!*

"At the time," he says, "I couldn't really explain my feeling about this, but it was basically that people did all these things—building careers, making money, buying cars and houses—*in order to be happy*. Why not cut to the chase and just go after happiness itself?"

Happiness itself as a vocation? Why not? The serious and thoughtful pursuit of happiness, it seems to me, calls for many of the same qualities as are required for success in any other quest: patience, self-knowledge, the strength and steadfastness to rebound from adversity.

In any case, the differing vocations of these two men put me in mind of the age-old argument about *being* versus *doing*.

The Eastern philosophies tend to espouse the primacy of *being*—of quiet contemplation, mindfulness, and the experience of connection and serenity; in a word, happiness. Western traditions tend to emphasize *doing*—achieving, accomplishing, leaving a mark; in a word, work.

Is one philosophy "better" or "truer" or "more useful"

than the other? The argument will never be settled. But I will say this: For a person with a true work-vocation, doing *equals* being. And, for a person with a sincere happiness-vocation, being *equals* doing. As far as I can tell, the conflict disappears.

Meanwhile, back at the piano, my ambivalent flirtation with my calling had entered yet another phase. I now had a friend named Lars, who shared my fascination with the keyboard. We started to play four-hand music together; a little later, we began writing and arranging our own songs.

This social aspect of music-making was new to me. I'd always viewed the piano as a solitary refuge. I was never in a band, and never wanted to be. Now the keyboard had become the focus of a friendship. Other kids played ball together or went fishing or wandered in the forest. Lars and I played music.

This was really nice—but, perhaps inevitably, it put yet another hurdle in my path. Lars and I were not overtly competitive—that's rarely how music happens—but still, I couldn't help comparing my playing to his, measuring my musical instincts and facility against my friend's. And I couldn't help feeling that my own ability was lagging.

Maybe this was fact; maybe it was just my insecurity. Human nature being what it is, the *accuracy* of my feeling made no difference. Either way, it put a crimp in my confidence and held me back from taking music very seriously. How could I even dream of making music my life's work when I was second-best relative to the only peer I had?

I would eventually find a way out of this dilemma—would come to understand, in fact, that it was a completely illusory and false dilemma. But it would take a few more years and a lot more self-doubt, some failed experiments, and a number of lucky coincidences before I reached that breakthrough.

One of the lucky coincidences—if it *was* a coincidence, as opposed to the exercise of my mother's mysterious wisdom—was the sudden appearance, one day when I was in high school, of a tape recorder in the Buffett home.

I've mentioned that I once repaired our portable phonograph with a sewing needle. That was a perhaps clumsy way of saying I had always had an interest in the confluence of music and technology. The tape recorder took that confluence to a whole new level. I saw it not just as a mechanical device, but as a magic box that held endless promise. I taught myself how to record a track, then dub another over it; then how to erase the first one and improve it. I was learning not just how to play music, but to *produce* recordings.

Make no mistake, this was pretty rudimentary stuff. Some kids mess around with chemistry sets; I was messing around with a piano and a tape recorder. But if the results were no great shakes, the process, I believe, was very important. Let me take a moment to explore this—because I believe it has application not only to the vocation of music, but to the search for one's personal niche in all sorts of fields.

Before the tape recorder was brought into the equation, I'm not sure I really understood how many different ways there are to be a musician. Being a musician equaled playing the piano and making up tunes. But the addition of technology made me realize that that definition was far too rigid and confining. Being a musician also included everything I could *do* with the playing and the melodies—first with the tape recorder, later in a studio.

In other words, making music was not a single skill or inclination, but a *complex* of skills and inclinations. Writing tunes was one such inclination; being comfortable with electronics was another. And the *combination* of those things began a process of refraction and multiplication, as in a hall of mirrors, so that the single concept of "musician" took on infinite shades of possibility—one of which might be right for me. Maybe I could find a way not just to make music, but to make *my* music.

How does this dynamic apply to other fields? Well, a case could be made that many, if not most, of us start off with an *inkling*, a rather general idea, of what our path should be; that inkling can become a true vocation only if we find a way to marry it to our specific *combination* of abilities and temperament—because it's in the combination, rather than the single traits or talents, that our uniqueness lies.

Say, for instance, that a person starts off with an inkling to become a doctor. But what *kind* of doctor should she be? If her temperament is of the leave-me-alone-with-my chemistry-set type, chances are she'd be happier and more effective—more *herself*—in a research setting than in treating patients. Similarly, the impulse to become a lawyer is awfully broad; but if that impulse is combined, say, with a passion for journalism, then maybe a concentration on First Amendment issues is the way to go.

In real life, of course, things are far more complicated than the preceding examples suggest. There aren't just *two* strands that determine our preferences; there may be dozens. Some will loom larger than others; some may be hidden from our conscious minds. Some may be in conflict with each other—an impulse toward personal satisfaction, say, as against a desire to make a lot of money.

But my point is this: However complex our personal web of preferences and talents and temperament may be, there will be some junction where the strands—or at least the most important strands—will intersect. If we are patient and open-minded and maybe a little bit lucky, we will eventually find our way to that point of intersection;

that's the place where our true vocation will lie waiting to be claimed.

Not that the combination of the piano and the tape recorder led me to that place in a flash of confidence and certainty. No, by the time I started college, I was still fumbling in the dark.

But the mind works in strange ways. We flatter ourselves that our thought processes are linear and clear. Doesn't always happen that way. Sometimes the mind plays tricks and works by sly indirection. Often it lags behind the heart. The heart *knows* things that the plodding mind then has to explain and justify by way of words and logic.

When I started Stanford, photography was still my main creative outlet. I took courses in it; I shot film constantly. I liked being the guy with the camera. At the same time, though, a certain frustration was setting in. After shooting thousands—maybe tens of thousands—of images, I could not say with confidence where the "art" was in my pictures. I could see that they were competent; I couldn't see what made them special. The camera itself, a mechanical device, stood between me and what I hoped to say. I couldn't see what made the pictures *mine.*

In retrospect, I think what was happening was that my

heart had already fallen out of love with photography, and my mind was trying to catch up. And here's where the slippery obliqueness came in: It seemed that I had to go through the painful loss of becoming disillusioned with photography before I could fully embrace my passion for music. It was like something out of a romantic comedy, when the protagonist finally realizes that his true love is not the flashy new woman who's entered his life, but the steadfast friend who's been there all along. That friend was the piano.

If I was getting tantalizingly close to acknowledging and seizing my life's calling, I wasn't quite there yet. Some stubborn issues remained. Confidence was one of them. Was I good enough? Would I *ever* be good enough?

Another issue was the complex and convoluted matter of family expectations. My parents had always encouraged me to find my bliss, to do whatever would make me feel fulfilled. They were sincere in this . . . but did they *really* mean it? (Read: Did *I* believe they really meant it?) Wasn't it simply human nature that parents would have their own preferences, their own dreams, for their kids? Would I be letting them down if I chose a field as out-of-the-mainstream, as uncertain, as music? Would I be "wasting" the privileged opportunity of a Stanford education if I opted for a field in which a degree was an irrelevancy?

Or was I just feeling guilty because feeling guilty is one of the many demon shapes that self-doubt can take?

In any case, it would require an overwhelming experience and a Eureka moment to finally sweep away my fears and qualms, and to make my decision seem not just clear, but inevitable.

One evening during my sophomore year of college, a friend invited me to his dorm to hear a visiting guitarist. This fellow's playing was amazing, and what was most remarkable about it was its simplicity. There was no showing off, no fiery or in-your-face technique, no complexity for the sake of complexity. But every note had a reason for being there. Every note was soulful and true. And I thought: *This is what music should be. And I can do this!*

I don't remember leaving that dorm room. I only remember finding myself back home, writing music in a kind of frenzy. I wrote two songs, then turned on the tape recorder and started overdubbing extra parts. I wrote and listened, added and subtracted, experimented and refined. I wanted no curlicues, nothing arbitrary.

I didn't sleep much that night. The next morning, a friend picked me up to drive to the beach. I took along a cassette of my new music and we listened to it as we drove.

When we got to the ocean, I had one of the strangest and most powerful experiences of my life. I opened the car door and found that I could not get out. I literally could not move. I was pinned to my seat by a new kind of gravity composed of equal parts responsibility and joy.

I realized that, on that short drive and through the tinny speakers of a secondhand, dirt brown Honda Civic, I had heard my future.

6

Buying time

Let's return, for a moment, to the notion of *privilege*—that decidedly mixed blessing that offers opportunity and comfort, but also complicates many lives and sometimes can even diminish them.

First of all, what do we mean when we talk about privilege?

The usual definition, of course, has to do with money and material advantages. But I would argue that a more inclusive definition is called for, because privilege can, in fact, take many forms.

A loving and supportive family is a privilege. So is the attention of caring teachers and mentors. Education is a privilege—and I'm not thinking only of book learning, but about education in the broadest sense; I'm talking about exposure to, and involvement with, a wide world filled with diverse people from many cultures—the kind of education that deepens our understanding and engages our empathy.

But what do all these different forms of privilege have in common?

For one thing, each of them *should* enhance our array of options in life; that potential enhancement is an essential part of what privilege is. But have you noticed that it doesn't always work out that way?

Privilege, I believe, is a two-edged sword. On the one hand, it can open up a world of possibilities; on the other hand, it tends to carry with it pressures—some external, some self-imposed—that can seriously circumscribe these possibilities.

Parental expectations constitute one such pressure. The influence of teachers and role models, even when the influence is positive, is a kind of pressure. Then there's social fashion—the pursuit of this year's hot career. Finally, the fact that we live in dicey economic times tends to push people toward the (seeming) security of the most mainstream work choices, the most-traveled paths.

For all these reasons, privileged people—whatever the exact form their privilege takes—sometimes seem to perceive their options as actually being *narrower* than most. This is unfortunate, even perverse; I also think it is undeniably true. Remember my Stanford acquaintance who seemed to have exactly two life-choices, doctoring or lawyering!

Privilege is like a telescope. If you look through one end, you can see a long way into a limitless universe; if you look through the other end, your world shrinks to a narrow swath. And since life is what we make it, the decision as to which way to turn the telescope belongs to each of us.

I mention this here because, just as privilege can either expand or limit our notions of choice, there is also a complex and sometimes paradoxical relationship between privilege and *time*.

Consider: Privilege of whatever sort *should* afford us the luxury of not hurrying through life. A measure of financial security should reduce the urgency to jump into the fray of making money. A supportive family will want to give its children time to find their bliss. Education should make us humble in the face of all the things we don't yet know; it should make us patient to learn more.

Privilege, then, should help us avoid rushing into big decisions or shortchanging each phase of our development because of a somewhat panicked impulse to get on to the next. As in the case of choices, privilege should give us *more* time, not less.

But you wouldn't know that by observing the behavior of many young people from privileged backgrounds. Are there any more hurried people on earth? They rush through prep school to get into the "right" college. They rush through college to impress the administrators of the "right" graduate programs. Their summers pass in a blur of internships that will look good on their résumés, that will get them a fast-track start at the bank or the brokerage or the law firm. No wonder some of these people have their so-called midlife crises at thirty or thirty-five; they've barely paused for breath since adolescence.

Let me make it clear that I say these things not in judgment but in solidarity. I understand that there are real and powerful pressures that push people toward this hurry-up approach to life. As has often been written, the current generation of young people is the first whose economic and professional prospects are, all in all, less rosy than those of their parents. The anxiety and frustration that go with this are entirely understandable. No one wants to be caught dawdling on the platform while the train is leaving the station; no one wants to miss out on the goodies at a time when the supply seems to be running short.

Still, I think we need to ask ourselves a couple very basic questions: Where is the line between, on the one hand, a positive, pragmatic, vigorous determination to *seize the moment,* and, on the other hand, a half-blind hurry driven not by joy or real commitment, but by the terrifying fear of being left behind? At what point in our rush through life do we give up more than we could possibly gain?

• • •

Allow me a brief excursion into nostalgia.

Back in the 1960s and '70s, when I was growing up, there was an emphasis put on the value of *finding oneself.* In support of this goal, people read *Siddhartha* and *On the Road;* they paused in their college careers to backpack around Europe or trek in Nepal. They allowed themselves breaks between college and grad school, between grad school and full-time employment. The aim was not simply to *fit in* with life, but to *find* the life that was the right fit for each of us.

Over time, of course, this notion of finding oneself went from being a quest to being a cliché; then it devolved into a punch line for a lot of bad jokes that portrayed the Baby Boomers as being a bunch of self-involved navel-gazers. And okay, the emphasis on finding oneself probably went too far; social trends always do, and that's why the pendulum swings.

Which is exactly my point: In recent years, I believe, the pendulum has swung too far the other way. In a world where everything from computers to economic cycles seems to be moving faster, we seem to regard introspection as a leisurely luxury we can no longer afford. Goaded by the fear of being left behind, we don't dare give ourselves the time to slow down and think.

But human nature doesn't change just because the

economy hurtles up or down, or because instantaneous texting takes the place of snail mail. As the old song says, "the fundamental things apply."

One of the fundamental things is that good decisions take time. They are processes, not spasms. They call for self-knowledge; and self-knowledge—like it or not!—calls for a certain amount of gut-checking or, if you prefer, navel-gazing. It calls for a certain amount of sitting still. (The word *Zen,* in fact, derives from a meditative practice called "za-zen," which literally means "just sitting.")

I can readily understand that, to a young person in a hurry, this quiet sitting might seem like a waste of time. But I'd like to propose a different way of looking at it. Pausing to look into one's own heart is never a *waste* of time; it's an *investment* of time, and in my view it's one of the most rewarding investments a person can make.

When I turned nineteen, as I've mentioned, I received my family inheritance. Technically, the gift came from my grandfather—proceeds from the sale of a farm he'd owned, and which my father had converted into Berkshire Hathaway stock. At the time I received them, the shares were worth roughly ninety thousand dollars. It was understood that I should expect nothing more.

So—what to do with the money? There were no strings attached; I could have done anything, the choice was mine. Buy a fancy car and move into an oceanfront condo? Fly around the world first-class? Fortunately, that kind of extravagance just wasn't me. Also, I'd had the advantage of seeing my older siblings burn through most of their cash rather quickly; I didn't want to follow that path.

At the other extreme, I might have done absolutely *nothing* with that stock—just left it in an account somewhere and forgotten about it. If I'd picked that option, my shares would now be worth around seventy-two million dollars. But I didn't make that choice, and I don't regret it for a second. People think I'm either lying or crazy when I say this, but it happens to be true, because I used my nest egg to buy something infinitely more valuable than money: I used it to buy time.

As luck would have it—or as life inevitably unfolds—my inheritance came to me just around the time I was finally committing to the pursuit of a career in music. As I hope is clear by now, the mere fact of making the commitment represented serious progress for me; it meant that I had, at least tentatively, come to terms with my own ambivalence, my own insecurity, my own concerns about the expectations of others. But if making the commitment was a necessary passage on the road to growing up, it was hardly a sufficient basis for launching a career. There was still so much I had to learn.

On the purely musical side, I was still working on my

piano technique, back in lessons for the fourth and—so far!—final time. On the producing side, I was struggling to keep up with recording technologies that were changing and expanding incredibly quickly. But neither my piano playing nor my gradually growing competence in the studio was an end in itself. Each of these separate but related skills was a means to a far more important and more elusive end: making the music my own.

My father and I used to talk about this. One of his favorite movies was *The Glenn Miller Story,* and one of his favorite aspects of it was the great bandleader's obsession with finding "the sound." This was the mysterious something that would make a Glenn Miller song or a Glenn Miller arrangement distinctive and immediately recognizable. This distinctiveness is a sort of Grail for many and maybe all musicians—think about Bob Dylan or Ella Fitzgerald—and, trust me, it does not come easily. (Even the sublime Ray Charles started his career as a sort of Nat King Cole imitator, before he became *Ray Charles.*)

Although finding "the sound" was a big job, even that was not the last piece of the puzzle. As a pragmatic Midwesterner with a limited nest egg, I knew that I would have to find a way to turn my creative impulses into a livelihood. But how did one do that? How would I find an audience, or clients, or a way to sell what I'd written and produced? The harsh truth is that, at that stage of the game, I didn't have a clue. But it was at least becoming clear to me that I wasn't going to figure it out by staying in a university, taking all those 101s and ologies!

I decided to leave Stanford and to use my inheritance to buy the time it would take to figure out if I could actually make a go of it in music.

With help from my father—yes, it's handy to have someone in the family who's good at this sort of thing!—I worked out a budget that would allow me to conserve my capital as long as possible. I moved to San Francisco, where I lived very frugally—small apartment, funky car. My sole extravagance was in updating and expanding my recording equipment.

I played the piano, wrote tunes, experimented with electronic sounds and overdubbing. Then I put a classified ad in the *San Francisco Chronicle,* offering to record all comers in my apartment studio.

And I waited.

The money I inherited from my grandfather was a relatively modest amount, but I am well aware that it was more than most young people receive to help them get a start in life. Having that money was a privilege, a gift I had not earned; I acknowledge it with gratitude. I acknowledge, as well, that if I'd faced the absolute necessity of making a living from day one, I would not have been able to follow the exact path I chose. I would have stuck with music—I was firm on that by now; but I probably would have sought a job in a recording studio. And who knows? I might have learned as much or more; might have become savvier, sooner, about the business side of music; might have made connections that could have accelerated my professional progress. Those are among the many things we'll never know about the paths we do not take.

In any case, the path I *did* take was one I'd chosen for myself. Again, I was privileged to be able to buy the time needed to explore that particular approach to a career. But the point I'd like to make here is this: There are *many* young people who are similarly privileged—either in terms of money or of emotional support or some unique opportunity or talent—yet who *don't* take advantage of the luxury of time, but barrel straight ahead into work lives that may or may not be right for them, that may or may not be fulfilling. Why do people do this?

I think there are two reasons. The first is that many people confuse the relative values of money and time.

Consider: Any economist will tell you that something that cannot be replaced is more valuable than something that can be. Money, as it turns out, is the only truly replaceable thing. Money is abstract; every dollar is like every other dollar. This is not to say that making money is easy, or that the lack of it isn't a serious concern. Nor do I mean to downplay the anxieties that crop up in harsh economic climates. But still, *money is replaceable.* You can have it today, lose it tomorrow, have it again the day after.

What else can you say that about? You can't replace a person or an experience; you can't precisely duplicate a sunset or a good hearty laugh. You can't reclaim even a single moment of your life once it's slipped away; wasted time is gone forever.

By that measure, it seems crystal clear that time is much more valuable than money. Yet people tend to live as though the opposite were true; as though tomorrow or next year are soon enough for self-knowledge and self-fulfillment, but money must come today. As if dreams can wait but a paycheck can't.

There are, of course, many situations in which a paycheck *can't* wait. If there is real urgency for basic needs, then making money, by necessity, *becomes* the best use of one's time.

But how do we define those "basic needs"?

This is a question that goes to the heart of the second reason many people don't take advantage of the gift of time: They have a distorted and inflated idea of what they *need,* as distinct from what they *want.*

If we really bring it down to basics, people need extraordinarily little. Henry David Thoreau, in *Walden,* after running through a catalog of the furniture and clothes and knickknacks with which people clutter up their lives, argues that true needs come down to two: food and warmth. But even this bare-bones description proves too uneconomical for Thoreau; he decides that food is only a means of providing "inner warmth." So that brings ultimate human needs down to one: maintaining body temperature!

Now, I don't know too many people who are willing to live as austerely as Thoreau, and I'm not suggesting we take his advice too literally. But the point, I think, is clear. Our absolute needs are few. And the more we *imagine* we need, the more we complicate our lives.

These phantom needs drive us to acquire; the urge to acquire dictates how we use our time, and thereby limits our freedom. The more we think we need, the less free we are; on the other hand, our freedom—our control of our own time—is increased by everything that we can do without.

But *doing without,* unfortunately, is something that many people don't seem to be so good at. Many people seem unwilling to live frugally; or, if they *must* live frugally, they see it as an affront, a penance that has been thrust upon them.

As I see it, though, living modestly—especially when we are young adults, essentially apprentices on the bumpy road to becoming masters of our own lives—is not a penance, but a salutary challenge. Being broke or close to it is a state of being entirely appropriate to a certain stage of life. It tests our ingenuity and our humor; it properly pulls our focus away from "stuff" and toward people and experience. It's not a tragedy!

Clearly, not all young people would agree with me on this. Part of the difficulty, I think, is that many simply don't know *how* to be frugal, how to do without; it's a life skill that they've never learned—and in this, it must be said, both their parents and society at large are complicit.

Which brings us to a ticklish subject. I don't like to sound negative or judgmental, but I am determined to keep these pages real and honest, and the plain truth is that there are a lot of spoiled kids out there. Many parents, with the most generous and loving intentions, have imbued their sons and daughters with questionable priorities and sometimes unrealistic expectations. This is part of the silver-dagger-in-the-back syndrome, and it has real consequences in terms of how these sons and daughters go on to define their own values, order their own lives, and decide how they will use their time.

If a boy grows up receiving lavish and expensive gifts for every Christmas and every birthday, it's only natural that he'll grow up associating those gifts with the love and security behind them (or, worse, see them as a proxy for security and love). Chances are that, as a young adult, he'll continue seeking comfort and reassurance in the goodies at the mall, and that he'll feel deprived, even diminished, if he can no longer afford them. If a girl grows up in a big, sunny bedroom, tidied by a housekeeper, it may be difficult for her to see the appropriateness and the advantage of sharing a cramped apartment with roommates on tight budgets.

In both these cases, there is a confusion between *needs* and *wants*; and the source of the confusion, at least in part, is the misguided generosity of parents that, in turn, creates a warped impression of what it is reasonable to expect from life—and when.

To state what should be obvious, it isn't reasonable or "normal" to live in luxury as a student or a young adult just going out into the world. Those are the years when we begin in earnest to make our lives our own; when we set out on the adventure of earning our own reward. If we hope to gain the self-respect that comes with independence, then it isn't realistic or even honest to imagine that, with barely a pause or a hiccup, we can continue to live in the manner of our affluent families.

In the normal course of things, rewards come *gradually*. That is part of the suspense and joy in life—that we sense ourselves moving forward, gaining in competence and knowledge, and being compensated for our progress, whether in money, or professional advancement, or creative satisfaction. Success, however we define it, happens little by little.

The process, in my view, should be savored. More is lost than gained if we try to hurry through it. But again, it comes down to a question of which we value more: money or time. Do we take the job with the signing bonus and the big starting salary because we feel the need for affluence from day one? Or do we live modestly so we can explore our options for the work we really want? (Or do we abdicate our independence altogether, and move back home, where the fridge is always full and our room gets cleaned by someone else?)

Do we take the quickest perceived path to the steaks and the champagne, or do we live on cottage cheese and apples for a while, as we give ourselves time to develop?

Personally, I've never known anyone to have been hurt by living for a while on cottage cheese and apples.

There's another nice thing about time: It's the medium in which luck can occur.

Luck, both good and bad, plays a part in every life—though people tend to imagine that the good luck is a consequence of personal merit, while the bad luck springs from some malevolent outside source. Be that as it may, luck generally takes time to find us. And we are in a better position to recognize and seize the luck if we've logged some effort getting ready for it. As Louis Pasteur said of his seemingly serendipitous scientific discoveries, "Chance favors the prepared mind."

In my own case, a bit of very important good luck

tracked me down one day in 1981, as I stood at a San Francisco curbside, washing my crummy old car.

At that point, I'd been living on my own for around two years. My carefully budgeted nest egg had tided me over to the point where I was beginning to make some money from my music. This wasn't yet a livelihood; my income was paltry, sporadic, and completely insecure. Still, I was doing enough and earning enough so that, privately at least, I felt I could claim the honorific title "working musician." Or at least *struggling* musician!

Part of the reason I was able to keep busy was that I would accept virtually any gig, even if it didn't pay. I wrote songs to learn the craft of writing songs. I wrote music for short films in order to explore the mysteries of matching music to picture, and using sound to advance a story. To me, these were fascinating challenges, not to mention survival skills for a fledgling composer.

I staked a bet on the growing interconnection between music and technology, upgrading my recording equipment whenever I could afford to, and also trying to stay current with the latest developments not only in audio technology, but in video as well. I treated each job sort of like a college assignment—worthwhile for what it had to teach; if there was a payday attached, so much the better.

Which brings us to that fortunate day in 1981.

Needing a break from the keyboard, I grabbed a bucket and some sponges and went outside to wash my dinged-up Volkswagen Rabbit. It was a mild, sunny day—a fairly rare event for San Francisco—and people were out strolling, gardening, or just sitting on their stoops. A neighbor with whom I'd had nothing more than a nodding acquaintance happened by. He stood there as I soaped and rinsed the car; I felt a little bit like Tom Sawyer whitewashing the fence.

We chatted, and in the course of conversation he asked me what I did for a living. When I told him I was a struggling composer, he suggested that I get in touch with his son-in-law, an animator who was always in need of music.

I followed up, met the son-in-law and his colleagues. It turned out that they did have work to offer me—though the nature of it, frankly, sounded pretty disappointing. They'd been commissioned to create ten-second "interstitials"—quick ads meant to flash a logo and help establish a brand—for a newly conceived cable channel.

Ten seconds? What could you compose that would take ten seconds and be any more than a fragment of a jingle?

Cable TV? Strange to tell, in 1981, cable was a fringe medium, not yet very widely distributed, its future by no means certain.

And a newly conceived channel, no less? Who knew if the thing would even launch, would ever see the light of day?

I took the work anyway, of course. And the cable channel more than launched; it rocketed to the moon. It was called MTV! It became the hottest thing going, one of the defining cultural phenomena of the 1980s.

Suddenly, *many* TV outlets wanted to look and *sound* like MTV. Advertisers wanted their products pitched with MTV-like imagery and music. Even films absorbed the influence, wanted something with that kinetic-electronic contemporary feel. Suffice it to say, I no longer had to take on unpaid work.

The moral of the story? Well, I could say that it pays to wash your own car; if I hadn't been living so frugally, I might have gone to a professional car wash and never met my neighbor!

But, seriously, the more important lesson, I think, comes back to the question of how we use our time.

If I had tried to rush my destiny—as if destiny could be rushed!—I would actually have been *less* prepared to recognize and exploit my lucky break. Without those hundreds of unpaid hours spent fiddling with my recording gear, I would not have found my own sound, my own approach. This required patience. Patience, in turn, required trust—a trust that good things would happen at their own natural pace. It would have been arrogant folly to imagine that I could force the tempo; I could only *get ready.*

Ready for what, exactly? I could not have said in advance. And this suggests another attitude that is very helpful if we are to make the best use of our time: humility. I had to acknowledge that, with my limited understanding and experience, I had no way of knowing what would happen next—or even, with any great exactness, what I *wanted* to happen next.

So, how much sense does it make to barrel through life full speed ahead before we're even quite sure where we really want to go?

7

Don't just find your bliss—*do* your bliss

Discovering a true vocation is a huge milestone on the way to making our lives what we want them to be. But it's only a first step.

Buying time to explore the implications and challenges of that vocation is also an important process. But it's only a second step.

The big question that remains is this: Once we've found our vocation, what do we *do* with it?

I am enough of a Midwesterner, and enough my father's son, to take a very pragmatic view of this question. If we want our vocations to become our livelihoods—rather than hobbies or vague dreams of things we'll get around to someday—then the hard and simple truth is that we have to find a way to make them pay.

This brings us to another of those delicate junctures where the pendulum of social fashion has swung, and swung again. I'm talking about how we regard the interplay between what we'd *like* to do and what we *need* to do. More precisely, I'm talking about the complex relationship between what we ourselves value, and what the outside world will pay us for.

Back in the 1960s and '70s, many young people tended to be obsessed and horrified by the notion of *selling out.* Any engagement with the marketplace was suspect; working for a big company or corporation was *highly* suspect. The idea seemed to be that by taking a "straight" job, or fulfilling a demand from a boss, or pleasing a client, we were necessarily being untrue to ourselves. And more than that: We were betraying the ideals and uniqueness of our entire generation.

With the benefit of some hindsight, it seems clear that the extreme individualism of the '60s, and the passion with which it was insisted upon, was a reaction against the equally extreme conformity of the '50s—the time of the Organization Man and the soulless commuter in the gray flannel suit. Who wanted to be like *that*?

The problem, of course, was that this horror of selling out overshot the mark of what was reasonable, and also overlooked some pretty basic economic realities. Even in better economic times, there were only so many livings to be made from producing tie-dyed clothing or selling incense or playing the tambourine!

In more recent years, under the stress of much dicier economic prospects, the pendulum has swung once more. These days, many people—seasoned professionals as well as those just entering the workforce—seem blithely unconcerned about selling out; instead, they tend to seem a bit frantic with the pressure of *buying in*. Rather than being suspicious of the marketplace, they are only too eager to embrace it, and to adopt its values without much questioning.

But what about their own values? Their own passions? Their own convictions about what constitutes a well-lived life?

When times are tough and the future looks murky, there is, I believe, a tendency to see one's own dreams and preferences as luxuries one can't afford. The immediate concern is to get a job, and keep it. While this attitude is entirely understandable, I don't think it holds up as a long-term formula for happiness and self-respect.

Let me be clear that I'm not advocating a return to "dropping out" and hippiedom. I accept and even celebrate the necessity of earning a living. Earning a living is one of life's character-defining challenges.

What I am trying to get across, however, is the idea of *balance*. If we hope to be true to ourselves, to fulfill our vocations while also paying the rent and putting bread on the table, we need to find the sweet spot where our individual abilities and inclinations intersect with the world of commerce. We need to figure out what it is we'd genuinely like to do . . . and that the world will value enough to buy.

Years ago, I happened upon a remark by the writer Bernard Malamud that has stayed with me all this time. Malamud was one of these fortunate—and extremely talented—people who seemed to have it all. His work was critically praised; his stories were published in prestigious magazines like *Esquire* and *The New Yorker.* Unlike a lot of "literary" writers, he was commercially successful, too. His novels made the best-seller lists; at least two of them, *The Natural* and *The Fixer*, were made into major studio films.

In an introduction to one of his short-story collections, Malamud remarked that "no good writer writes exactly as he pleases."

This was such a simple, quiet sentence that I read right past it—until I reflected on it and realized what a startling comment it really was.

No good writer writes exactly as he pleases.

Please bear with me as I try to parse this statement, because I think there's something quite important here. What Malamud was saying, I believe, is that it's a myth to imagine that a professional writer, however gifted or experienced, simply sits down at the keyboard and lets the words flow. No, there's another step involved, a mediation. There's the author's impulse, which is passionate; then there's a consideration of the potential audience, which is practical; and the finished piece of work is the offspring of those two factors.

Note that I don't call it a compromise; it is not a compromise.

Rather, it represents the application of several different skills, each of which is an integral part of Malamud's talent. Aside from what we think of as the purely "creative" aspect, there's the clarity required to understand the marketplace, and the discipline and skill needed to bring one's vision to an audience. Malamud uses all those talents to find his artistic and commercial sweet spot—and, most impressively, he does it *while always sounding exactly like himself, and no one else.*

Now, if this dynamic applied only to writers, or only to "creative types" more generally, it might not be worth analyzing here. But I happen to believe that Malamud's statement holds an important lesson for *all* of us—or certainly for anyone who hopes to turn a passionately held vocation into a livelihood.

The lesson, put simply, is this. When we do something for pay, whether it's writing a story or digging a ditch, we need to please the person paying us; *but that doesn't make the work any less our own.*

The paradox is that the finished product, whatever it

happens to be, belongs to us as much as to the buyer. We've put our own stamp on it; we've brought our uniqueness to it. Because it is part of *what we've done,* it has become a part, as well, of *who we are.*

Accepting this paradox—of selling something and yet still possessing it—is part of how we become professional. It's part of how we segue from finding our bliss to *doing* our bliss.

My entrée into the world of professional composing was as a writer of music for TV commercials. Advertising, of course, is a field in which creativity and commerce are thoroughly, completely intertwined. In fact, the motto of one of the great pioneering ad agencies, Benton and Bowles, was "It isn't creative unless it sells." This sentiment may drive certain purists crazy, but hey, welcome to reality.

There were many useful lessons to be learned from writing for commercials, and most of them were very humbling. Probably the most basic lesson was this: I had to acknowledge and accept the fact that I was working in a service industry. My music was not an end in itself. It was part of a larger conception, and that larger conception was not intended as a work of art, but as a tool for selling a product.

Understand, I say this not as a put-down or an apology;

as with everything else in life, writing for commercials can be done well or done badly; and when it's done well it takes on dignity and stature. Still, the reality was that I was there to serve the client; accepting this—really getting it—was a big part of becoming a professional, of turning a vocation into a livelihood.

As a corollary to this most basic lesson, I also had to accept that my music, which I poured my heart and soul into, was rarely the most important part of the commercial package. The product was the most important part by far. Next came the imagery—since TV, after all, is primarily a visual medium. A fresh concept or catchy slogan probably came after that. *Then* there was the music. In the best case, the music played an important supporting role, setting the tone or establishing an attitude; in the worst case, it was simply filler or an afterthought.

But here's something I learned, and that I believe has application for every working person in every field: No matter how important the music was or wasn't, I had to approach it *as if it were the most important part of the process.*

There were two reasons for this. The first was self-respect. As we've seen, there's a paradox when you do something for pay: You sell it, and yet it remains a part of who you are. If I coasted on a job, if I allowed myself to believe that my contribution didn't really matter much, I wouldn't just be shortchanging the client—I'd be doing myself a disservice. I'd be putting something out there that was less than the best I could do, and even if nobody noticed except for me, there would be a certain diminishment in the falling-short. A lazy piece of work would linger as a personal embarrassment.

The other reason for always behaving *as if* one's work is all-important is more practical: It's the best and maybe the only way to grow as a professional. Life is school; every gig is an opportunity to learn. Every challenge presented by the world offers us a chance to hone our skills and bring our perceptions into clearer focus.

I have a sort of Buddhist image that applies, I think, in this connection: sharpening a knife. The knife is each of us. The outside world, with its demands and expectations, is the whetting stone, the grinding wheel. The only way we can keep our edge is to submit to the friction of the stone. This takes a certain courage, because the stone is huge and its grinding is relentless; it also takes a certain humility, an understanding that the wheel will keep on turning long after our own little substance has been all used up. To get the greatest benefit, the keenest edge, from the collision of knife and wheel, a certain mix of passive and active is called for. We have to surrender ourselves to the friction of the wheel; but we also have to hold our ground, mindfully position ourselves at the proper angle and with the proper firmness, so that the steel rings, sparks fly—sparks of creativity and passion and commitment—and we come away improved and refreshed.

But okay, in the literal, day-to-day world of work, the friction that makes the sparks fly comes not from a grinding wheel, but from our interactions with other people. This is because working for pay necessarily implies a relationship—in fact, a whole matrix of relationships. And the way we deal with those relationships—with bosses, colleagues, clients—goes a long way toward determining not only our level of professional success, but also the degree of comfort with which we're able to balance the sometimes conflicting demands of ego and career.

Let me try to illustrate some aspects of this dynamic by example.

I tend to be extremely self-critical; I'm seldom if ever entirely satisfied with anything I've done. But sometimes, in my early writing for commercials, I would come up with a tune or a sound that I just plain fell in love with; I'd go into a meeting with the client, feeling entirely confident that I had nailed it.

And sometimes the client didn't like what I'd done. Sometimes the client *hated* it! Sometimes the client thought that the exact part I was in love with was the part that didn't work.

Well . . . how does one deal with a situation like that (other than by gritting one's teeth and getting a bellyache)? Human nature being what it is, there's a probably universal impulse to react defensively. *I know I'm right! That guy must really be a jerk!*

An understandable response, but where does it get you? In the short term, it probably gets you fired. More important, in the longer term, it deprives you of an opportunity to learn.

Maybe the client *isn't* a jerk. Maybe he understands things about the business that you have yet to figure out. Maybe he has a broader perspective than you have yet to attain. And maybe, if you truly open up and listen to what he has to say—rather than getting defensive and insulted—maybe the process will make you better at what you do.

Again, what's called for in situations like this is one of those balancing acts on which so much of our happiness and self-respect depends. We have to balance ego against the legitimate demands of working relationships. Our lives are our own; our work is our own; but to a considerable extent, it is the outside world that defines us. If we don't openly and honestly consider the feedback we're getting from the world, how can we really know how we're doing—if we're accomplishing anything of value? If we're accomplishing anything at all?

So, for example, I had to learn that my own enthusiasm

for a song or a musical conception—while it was a necessary part of doing a job well—was not the be-all and end-all. Other people had to love it, too. And if they didn't, I had to be prepared to change it or to stick it in a drawer and start over.

But here's the thing. I found that if I didn't resist the feedback, if I didn't succumb to frustration or hurt feelings, I almost always ended up with something better than I had started with.

And I also realized that I owed a debt of gratitude to the clients and colleagues who led me to the eventual finished music, even when the path to it was rocky. Listening to them—honoring our relationship—had made me better.

Writing music is essentially a solitary activity. A tune or a rhythm or a pattern mysteriously forms in the composer's mind, resolves itself into notes that can be played on a keyboard or written on a staff—and only then can it be shared with others.

But if composing is solitary, composing *for a living* is necessarily collaborative. This is yet another paradox, another potential source of conflict or frustration at the point where the self rubs up against the outside world. When does a piece of music cease being *mine* and become *theirs*? How do I deal with the often painful process of letting it go? Freud would call the desire to hold on an example of infantile anal retentiveness. Maybe so, maybe not. But the tug of it is undeniable. The conflict is this: Once I've created something, I don't like other people to mess with it; but once I've *sold* something, other people have an entirely legitimate stake in it.

How can we resolve this conflict?

In the early years of my career, I used to dread those inevitable moments when a client would be standing next to me, literally looking over my shoulder as I sat at the keyboard, and would ask me to "Come up with something for this" or "Give us something sort of Latin for that" or suggest "How about something more upbeat over here."

Faced with this barrage of input and pressure of expectation, I would feel a wave of anxiety that I tried my best not to show. But my mouth would go dry; my mind would go blank; I'd look down at the familiar keyboard and for a moment it would seem like a stranger. Usually I'd manage to come up with something suitable—that was my job, after all—but the process was agony.

Over time, it became easier. Why? Because, by experience rather than by conscious thought, I'd undergone a simple but profound attitude adjustment. In the early years, when I was asked to compose on the fly, I'd see the process as a duality. *I* was being asked to perform, while *she*—the client—was making demands. *I* was being asked to create, while *she* was ready to judge.

With more experience and gradually growing confidence, however, I came to understand that my way of looking at this was neither productive nor accurate. When it came to the task at hand, it wasn't a case of *I* and *she*. The point was that *we* were trying to get something done *together.* We were teammates, not adversaries; I needed to respect her contribution to the process. But in order to do that, I needed to relax, to conquer my own insecurity.

I needed to understand that my work was still my own—maybe even *more* my own—when I yielded my sole claim to it and allowed it to become collaborative.

I stress this dynamic and this transition because I happen to believe that *all* work is, first and foremost, solitary effort. Even the most apparently seamless teamwork starts with individuals doing their very best, and then making common cause with their fellow workers.

Have you ever watched the full credits that roll at the end of a movie? *Hundreds* of people have labored to bring that film to the screen; a more thoroughly collaborative project can hardly be imagined. Still, *at the moment of performing their separate tasks,* each and every person has worked alone. Every person has put something of him- or herself into the product; every person has a stake of professionalism and pride.

As it is on a film set, so it is in a school or a clinic or a foundation—in any setting where a number of people work *both separately and together* to accomplish a goal that encompasses the passions and aspirations of them all.

Through cooperation and teamwork, people can do things that are bigger and grander than any individual; but the teamwork comes together only if people bring their uniqueness and their special talents to the effort.

Each person gives something. And each person still owns what he or she has given.

This realization is, I believe, a crucial bridge between *finding* our bliss and *doing* our bliss.

Finding our bliss is essentially a journey of self-discovery. Where do our talents lie? What are the things we truly care about? What pursuits allow us to feel that we are being truest to ourselves, living the lives that we were meant to live?

Doing our bliss entails a somewhat different sort of journey—a journey *beyond* ourselves. These talents and abilities we've discovered—how do they connect with the world outside our skin? What does the world *need* from us? Where is the all-important intersection between the things we value in ourselves, and the things the world will value from us?

Finding that intersection is one of life's great challenges. And if we are fortunate enough to locate it—and even more fortunate to be able to earn our livings there—then that gives us our very best chance at fulfillment in our work.

8

Portals of discovery

A man of genius makes no mistakes. His errors are volitional and are the portals of discovery.

James Joyce wrote that, in reference to Shakespeare. Maybe it's true when it comes to geniuses; who knows? But the rest of us make *plenty* of mistakes—and not intentionally, either. We make mistakes because we're human.

We make mistakes because of knowing too little; we make mistakes because of imagining we know more than we do.

We make mistakes when we neglect the importance of a moment; we make mistakes when we think *only* of the moment.

We make mistakes when we become impatient; equally, we make mistakes when we are indecisive. There are foolish acts; there are foolish failures to act.

We make mistakes out of boldness; we make mistakes out of timidity. We make mistakes when we are overly ambitious and when we are not ambitious enough.

We make mistakes when we let our actions become detached from our values.

Just as mistakes come from many causes, they come in all shapes and sizes. There are tiny gaffes that embarrass us for a moment or two; there are major blunders that fill us with chagrin and remorse for years or even decades. But whatever their origin and whatever their scale, there is one thing that all our errors have in common: They are opportunities to learn.

They are portals of discovery—not only for geniuses, but for the rest of us as well.

When we come up with a wrong answer to one of life's innumerable questions, we are at least one step closer to a right answer—or at least the answer that's right for us. When we let ourselves down by inattention or lack of conviction, the twinge we feel is a healthy reminder to maintain our standards and our vigilance. When we goof, and confront the consequences of our goofing, we have the opportunity to figure out what *doesn't* work, and why.

In short, we grow by messing up.

I stress this because I've observed that, especially in

difficult or uncertain times, many people seem terribly afraid of making mistakes—as if a mistake were a personal humiliation from which one would never recover, the dreaded "black mark" on the permanent record.

But that's just not how it is. Mistakes are very seldom permanent; most of them can be fixed with less difficulty and drama than one imagines, and there's nothing shameful about making them. There is, however, something sad and limiting about the *fear* of making them.

If we let ourselves be controlled by the fear of stumbling, we can walk only the widest, most-trod paths. If we refuse to cut ourselves some slack for messing up, then we'll be disinclined to take chances; and if we don't take chances, we may never find our passion or our truest selves. If we're afraid that the beat of our own drummer might lead us to a misstep, then we can only march along with everybody else.

And you know what? Even if we play it as safe as we possibly can, we'll make mistakes anyway! Everybody does. Mistakes are inevitable. They're part of life.

If life is what we make it, and if we want our lives to be vivid and authentic, then we have to accept the fact that we will mess up now and then along the way. We can't eliminate errors, so we may as well embrace them. Admit them when they happen, forgive ourselves for making them, and most of all, learn from them.

No mistake should go to waste!

• • •

Let me tell you a story about two brothers.

They grew up in California, in comfortable though not wealthy circumstances. Their father was an engineer who worked for a private firm under contract to NASA. Their mother was a teacher who suspended her career during their childhoods, then became a tutor in English as a second language.

But it was engineering that seemed to set the template for appropriate careers. The father had worked for the same company for decades; he had stability, security, paid vacations, benefits. He worked hard, but for the most part, he seemed blessedly free of the stresses and uncertainties that go with many professions. Moreover, he still seemed to get a kick out of what he did for a living. He would talk with almost childlike enthusiasm about the extraordinary elegance of an airplane wing or the mind-boggling thrust of a rocket engine.

The sons seemed to inherit some but not all of the father's abilities. They were both very bright; math and science came especially easily to them. In terms of academic leanings, they seemed perfectly suited to follow in their father's footsteps and become engineers.

But something was missing. That something was passion. For the father, engineering was exciting and fulfilling. For the sons it was simply the default mode, the expected choice. It seemed the safest option, the path least likely to lead to a mistake.

One of the brothers, Jeff, eased onto that more trodden path and became an electrical engineer. This was during the 1990s, and electrical engineering was a very good ticket to have. He went to work for a software company and started making a very nice living. He didn't love his work; he didn't hate it. It was just what he did. It was fine.

The other brother, Dan, resisted the tug of the expected choice. He wasn't really sure what he wanted to do. This caused his family a lot of anxiety and caused Dan a lot of difficulty. He didn't stick with things; he kept changing his mind. *He made mistakes.* He got an engineering degree but then didn't want to use it. He flirted with the idea of becoming a chef, but came to feel that, although he was fascinated by the inner workings of restaurants, it wasn't the food itself that held his interest. Great—so now he had a degree he wasn't using and some work experience he didn't care to follow up on. Mistakes and more mistakes!

The millennium came, the dot-coms crashed, and Jeff, the more reliable brother, lost his job. This was not his fault; like so many other people, he was caught in an economic downdraft that no one had been able to foresee or seemed able to control. Still, getting that pink slip demanded a reevaluation of many of the choices Jeff had made.

"It was a difficult but really interesting process," he says of this reevaluation. "My first thought was that my mistake was getting fired. That was only natural, right? One day I had a job, next day I didn't. Losing the job was where I goofed. But then I realized that wasn't it at all. Getting fired wasn't the mistake; that was only the occasion for *considering* the mistake. The real mistake was taking that job in the first place.

"Why did I take it? I was never that excited about it. I took it because I imagined it was safe. Because it would save me the trouble and anxiety of thinking too much about other possibilities. My mistake was in imagining I could avoid mistakes!"

A painful acknowledgment. But again, mistakes are temporary setbacks, not permanent disasters; course corrections rather than defeats. And if there's any good news about an economic downdraft—whether it's the dot-com crash or the financial crisis of more recent years—it's that tough times force many people into necessary reevaluations that lead in the long term to more fulfilling lives.

Out of work, Jeff had time to think about what he liked and didn't like about his former job. He liked the science; he was genuinely pumped about the possibilities of technological innovation. He didn't like sitting in a cubicle, communing with machines instead of people.

With this awareness—earned by way of his previous "mistake"—he rebounded onto a new trajectory. He applied to law school and has since become a patent attorney. He uses his science background; he works closely with people in the service of innovation. It's a perfect synthesis for him—but to get there, he had to do a clear and honest analysis of where he'd gone wrong in the first place.

And what about the other brother—the one who seemed to be blundering from engineering school to the restaurant business and out again? He also found his synthesis by way of things that hadn't quite worked out.

The engineering curriculum didn't really satisfy his creative, independent side. His foray into the food industry showed him that he didn't have the temperament to be a chef. Working in restaurant kitchens, though, he found himself thinking like an engineer. He saw each kitchen as a kind of factory, each appliance and tool as a cog in a production process. How could the factory be made to work most efficiently? How could time and energy be saved? How could safety be improved, how could kitchen staff be best protected against burned fingers and sore backs?

Dan came to realize that his false starts and meanderings had given him a fairly rare and useful skill set. He could make schematic drawings; he understood the science of heat and of materials. He knew *firsthand* how heavy commercial saucepans were, how crucial the spacing of a kitchen line.

He became an industrial designer, specializing in commercial kitchens. He had blundered his way to exactly where he was meant to be.

• • •

But okay, if I'm talking about mistakes, it seems only fair that I fess up to a few of my own. Fortunately, I have plenty to choose from!

I'll start with a mistake that is really a classic—by which I mean that lots of other people made this same error before me. I'd heard of other people making this mistake. I'd *seen* other people make this mistake. (For that matter, variations on this same blunder, repeated on a global scale, would later come pretty close to wrecking the world financial system!) But in the actual event, it didn't seem to matter what I'd seen or what I thought I knew. I made the mistake anyway.

This points out something fundamental about many of our goofs. We might think we understand how they happen, that we are savvy about where the pitfalls lie. But we don't *really* understand mistakes until we've made them for ourselves.

Benjamin Franklin famously observed, "Experience keeps a dear school, but a fool learns in no other." If that's true—and who am I to disagree with Ben Franklin?—then *all* of us are fools. That's why even the wisest and best-intentioned advice is simply that—advice, and not some foolproof preventive medicine.

Be that as it may, the mistake I want to examine here is my classic Big House blunder.

This brings me back to the late 1980s. I was cruising

along in my business of writing music for commercials, finally making a pretty good living. I'd gotten married, and along with my wife at the time came beautiful twin girls. So there I was—a reasonably successful composer, as well as a husband and father. It seemed like a logical time to become a homeowner as well. The opportunity presented itself for me to buy the house we were living in, in San Francisco, and I went for it.

So far, so good. I could afford that house without too much of a stretch. Its scale was appropriate for the needs of my family.

The next move was the one that got me into trouble.

Hoping to expand my musical horizons, I'd signed on with a record label called Narada, based in Milwaukee. This association would enable me to market and distribute my own CDs. It would also expand my producing work, as other artists on the label would be encouraged to record in my studio. Finally, the arrangement carried with it the vague but spiffy-sounding job title of executive producer. The opportunity, coupled with my Midwest roots, which still ran pretty deep, persuaded me to pull up stakes and move to Milwaukee.

The first order of business, though, was to sell the San Francisco house. Here I got lucky—or so it seemed at the time. The Bay Area was experiencing one of its cyclical booms in housing prices, and I was able to sell relatively quickly, painlessly, and at a considerable profit.

If this was good news, it was also a snare. It launched me on a series of small errors that eventually coalesced into a Big Mistake.

Error number one: Since my very first foray into the buying and selling of houses had been a triumph, I thought, *Well, that was easy!*

Error number two: Since it's part of human nature to imagine we've been smart when in fact we've just been fortunate, I allowed myself the vanity of thinking, *Hmm, maybe I have a feel for this real estate stuff . . .*

The errors continued at the Milwaukee end of the transaction. Compared with the Bay Area, metro Milwaukee seemed incredibly affordable, and I thought, *Why not make a really big investment now, and cash in when Wisconsin prices boom, just like they had in San Francisco?*

In retrospect, I was sort of setting up shop as a one-man real estate bubble. I thought prices could only go up. I thought that aggressive if not reckless investments in houses couldn't possibly lose.

So I bought a really big house, right on Lake Michigan. It was probably five times the size of our place in San Francisco. It had space for a great studio and extra rooms to put up visiting artists. It was way out of my price range—or what my price range *should* have been; upkeep was enormous and unending, but what the heck. The property would certainly appreciate, and in the meantime, my career was clearly on the upswing . . . right?

But again, this seemingly rational line of thought was riddled with misjudgments.

Why didn't I realize that my business would experience a hiccup or two with the move? Writing for commercials was still my bread and butter, and, as I've mentioned, that put me in a service industry. I had to work harder and travel more often to service clients I'd had in San Francisco. Some of them, inevitably, drifted away.

Regarding my fancy in-home studio, the idea was that other Narada artists would want to record there, thus defraying costs. But what if they didn't?

And what about this executive producer stuff? I'd liked the sound of it, but faced with the reality I was reminded that I was a freelancer at heart. I didn't like sitting at a desk, dealing with other people's issues. I didn't like having other people to answer to.

Bottom line, I found myself way over my head with house payments. I was saddled with more work-related stress than I had ever felt before, and I was getting to do less, not more, of what I really wanted to do.

Why had I done this to myself? How had it happened?

The answer, I believe, has application to the hows and whys of *many* of the big mistakes that people make.

Basically, I think I made my big house blunder because I confused reasons with justifications.

At each step of the way, I could marshal arguments for why buying a really big house made sense. I *had* made money on the San Francisco sale. Milwaukee *was* a relative bargain. And so on.

But none of those arguments was a before-the-fact *reason* to buy a big house. Rather, they were after-the-fact justifications for doing what I felt like doing. Because the simple facts were these: I really wanted to move back to the Midwest. I fell in love with a beautiful piece of property. *And, at that stage of my life, I just plain wanted a big house!*

Why was this important to me? The reasons are complicated and murky and largely hidden from me even now. Probably they were quite ordinary reasons. Perhaps, misguidedly, I saw owning a big house as a passage to full adulthood. Perhaps, misguidedly again, I needed a visible token of my professional progress.

Whatever my precise motivation, the significant thing, I think, was this. I kidded myself that I was being entirely rational, when in fact I was being driven by wants and pressures quite removed from rationality.

And that's how a lot of big mistakes happen.

Was my big house mistake naïve? Yes. Was it avoidable? Maybe. Am I embarrassed about it years later? Absolutely not.

This brings me back, full circle, to the set of ideas that opened this chapter. Mistakes are inevitable, so we may as well accept them, forgive ourselves, and move on. Our errors may cause us inconvenience, might cost us time and money, but—assuming they are *honest* errors—they are not shameful. Every blunder is a learning opportunity, a marker on the winding road of where we've been, where we are, and where we think we're headed.

If, out of fear of being left behind, or of making some misstep from which we won't recover, we deny ourselves the slack to make mistakes, then we deprive ourselves of those opportunities to learn. Worse, when we *do* make mistakes but refuse to admit them, out of stubbornness or insecurity or inattention, we miss the chance to bounce off the error and head in some better direction.

We miss the chance to become better at being who we are.

Here is yet another of those paradoxes that I seem to run into whenever I try to express in simple words something true and basic about life: We are, and are not, the same people we were yesterday.

There is, of course, a continuity in who we are. That's how we recognize our faces in the mirror every morning, how we recall the kinds of things that make us laugh, how we maintain loyalty and steady affection in our relationships.

But it's equally true that we are always changing, developing, evolving. Each day we know a little more about the world and a little more about our own minds and hearts.

The mistakes we have made, and the course corrections that resulted from those blunders, are an essential part of our evolution. So, if we hope to feel good about the people we are *now*, we need to regard with candor and acceptance the people we were *then*—when we made those dumb mistakes!

So, for example, when I think back to my Big House error, I acknowledge that my decision-making was faulty, that my spasm of desire for a fancy home was a straying from my truer values. I don't disown the blunder, but I look at it almost as if the folly had been committed by a different person—a younger friend. Rather than feel embarrassed about my naïveté then, I can take satisfaction in the things I've learned and the ground I've covered since.

Not that I pretend to have outgrown or outrun my capacity to make mistakes. I still make my share of blunders, and some of them, at some point in the future, will no doubt seem as much of a head-scratcher as the Big House mistake seems to me today. I know that I'll have many more occasions to look back and say to myself, *Pete, what were you thinking?*

Confronting that question can sometimes be a little galling. But trying to answer it truthfully is always a worthwhile exercise.

9

Be careful what you wish for...

. . . because you just might get it.

This Chinese proverb, in my view, holds an extraordinary kernel of wisdom—a wisdom that cuts straight to the core of human nature and therefore seems to apply to all cultures and in all times.

Consider the Greek legend of King Midas. Obsessed with gold, Midas wished for more and more of it; in fact, he wished to be able to turn *everything* to gold. This rash and dangerous wish was granted, in the form of the famous "Midas touch." For a brief time, the king was happy with his newfound power and boundless wealth . . . until he touched his beloved daughter, who was promptly changed from a loving, laughing human being into a lifeless golden statue.

After all these centuries, the Midas story still rings true and packs a punch. Why? Two reasons, I think. The first is that it is a perfect illustration of the serious and sometimes tragic irony of life. A longed-for gift becomes a terrible burden. The fulfillment of a fantasy turns into a disaster. But note: This cruel irony doesn't just *happen* to Midas; he brings it about himself. This is a story about human nature, not the wrath of the gods. Midas's irony comes from *within*—from a basic confusion between what he *thinks* will make him happy, and what is truly important in his life.

The second reason the Midas story still speaks to us across the centuries is that it remains a resonant if painful metaphor of one of the dangers facing wealthy parents. What happens to the kids if the parents put the pursuit of money above all else? Are they, in some figurative sense, turned into golden statues?

This is a question we'll return to in due course. For now, however, let's consider some other instances of wishes being granted—and of the unforeseen consequences that ensued.

I know a man who had a long and mostly happy career as an editor of a glossy national magazine. He started as an assistant, answering phones and making coffee while learning the rudiments of the business. Then, over the course of twenty years, he moved up through the ranks.

His rise was not flashy or meteoric, but slow and steady, based on growing expertise and a network of colleagues who were, in turn, rising to more senior positions. At length he was promoted to executive editor, the number two spot on the masthead.

This, as it happened, was the perfect job for him. As executive editor, he had discretion to choose writers and assign stories; he also had time to do the hands-on editing, shaping articles and making them better. Those were things he was really good at; equally or maybe even more important, those were things he *liked doing.*

As for the job of editor in chief, that called for a somewhat different temperament and entailed a different set of tasks. The editor in chief was responsible for budgets and had to deal with the corporate politics of the parent company. He was the public face of the magazine and had to spend a lot of time entertaining and making official appearances. As at most magazines, the editor in chief had little or no time left over to actually edit.

"I loved being number two," my acquaintance recalls. "I loved being able to sit quietly in my office with a manuscript. I loved having that layer of insulation between me and the suits."

But then the editor in chief decided to retire, and the formerly contented number two started wishing for the top job. Why?

"The promotion carried a substantial raise," this fellow says, "but it wasn't really about the money. It was more about ego. I wanted finally to see my name in bigger type at the top of the masthead. And it was also about how I'd feel if I *didn't* get the job. I'd feel dissed, humiliated. And if I was passed over, it would be a public embarrassment—or public within the industry at least."

All those feelings are understandable, I guess; unfortunately, though, they have almost nothing to do with the day-to-day reality of being editor in chief of a magazine. So my acquaintance was putting himself in the perverse but entirely human position of wishing for something that, in fact, would not make him happy.

For better or worse, his wish was granted. He got the job and the raise and the corner office. He also got a lot of bellyaches and sleepless nights. He resigned after two frustrating and stress-filled years.

Could this story have had a happier ending? In theory, sure. This fellow could have taken himself out of the running for the editor in chief position and made it clear that it was his choice to stay on at number two. But how many people would really have done that?

Again, it seems to be an ingrained facet of human nature to confuse what we *really* want with what we *think* we want. Add to that tendency the social pressure that goes with what we think we *should* want—a raise, a promotion, public recognition—and it becomes extremely challenging to make decisions in accordance with our happiness, rather than with our sometimes misguided wishes.

Our society eggs us on to reach for the brass ring, whether we want the silly thing or not! It's a rare person who can resist the temptation and the pressure.

I don't know how many people remember the name Louis Lefkowitz. For more than a decade during the 1960s and '70s, he served as attorney general of New York State. A man of impeccable integrity, he served with equal success under Democratic and Republican governors. For all his time in public office, he seemed to have no enemies, no detractors. When Nelson Rockefeller died in office, Lefkowitz was asked to become lieutenant governor, in preparation for his own run at the state's top office. Everyone seemed to agree he would win in a landslide.

Lefkowitz turned down the promotion. He already had the job that was right for him, the job he really enjoyed. He simply shrugged off the idea of becoming governor, saying to the press, "Why take a job you don't really want? Why be unhappy?"

This bit of candor and wisdom was regarded as so refreshingly unusual that the *New York Times* featured it on the top of page one, as the quote of the day.

But really, why should Lefkowitz's attitude seem so rare? *All* of us, in our various ways, face the choice of pursuing a higher rung of the ladder, or not. Most people, it seems, are inclined to keep chasing the *next* wish.

But maybe the happier people—the ones most in sync with their own lives—are the ones who recognize and honor and savor the wishes that have *already* come true.

The dangers of wishing take many forms.

One of them is that wishing can sometimes pose as a substitute for *preparation*. Serious wishing, after all, takes a lot of energy, a lot of focus. It's understandable, therefore, that people sometimes kid themselves that hoping something will happen is the same as getting ready to deal with it when it does.

These are two different things!

Wishing is not the same as preparing. Hoping is not the same as getting ready. I say this on good authority, because one of the biggest blunders of my own professional life came from the confusion of these concepts.

Some backstory is in order. I've mentioned that, when I left San Francisco and moved to Milwaukee, part of my motivation was the desire to expand my musical horizons. I still enjoyed writing for commercials—and I certainly enjoyed getting paid for it. But I was beginning to chafe at the limitations of the form; some of my musical thoughts, after all, needed more than thirty seconds to express! Also, as I got a little older and as the novelty of professional acceptance started wearing off, I began to be dogged by the question of what my music was *for*. Did it exist merely to help sell a product? Wasn't there some higher purpose the music could be serving? Wasn't there some layer of meaning and fulfillment that was way beyond what I had experienced so far?

From questions like these, and from my growing restlessness, a wish was born: I wished for the opportunity to write for film.

This wish, I suppose, was presumptuous, though not entirely without foundation. Through my writing for commercials, I had learned the craft of matching music to pictures; on a tiny scale, I was already using music to advance a narrative. True, it was quite a leap to go from a thirty-second commercial to a two-hour feature film, but that was okay, because a leap into the unknown was exactly what I was hankering for.

The only problem, of course, was how to make it happen.

The conventional wisdom held that if you wanted to work in the movies, in whatever capacity, you needed to move to L.A. That's where the connections got made, where the deals were done. If you wanted to break into the entertainment business, you put in your time at the meetings and the parties; you networked and you schmoozed. You didn't burst on the scene from an outpost two time zones away.

But here I learned a lesson from my father—not so much a conscious lesson as a temperamental affinity. When my father started Berkshire Hathaway, New York—even more than today, when things have become relatively decentralized—was the absolute center of the financial world. If you wanted a career on "Wall Street," you *went* to Wall Street, period.

My father saw it otherwise. Instinctively, he grasped the dangers of group-think. Too many people chasing the same thing in the same place seemed to lead, inevitably, to muddled reasoning and a herd mentality. Jargon took the place of real ideas; knowing who was who became a poor substitute for knowing what was what. The old cliché had it that the cream would rise to the top, but in fact it was probably just as true that most people got homogenized. So my father stayed in Omaha and did things his own way, trusting to his own ideas and methods.

By a somewhat similar mental process, I decided to skip Los Angeles and move to Milwaukee. I was hoping to develop my own sound, my own brand. How could I do that if I was chasing the same jobs as everybody else, trying to write in this month's fashionable style or to ape the success of a recently successful soundtrack?

Not that I turned my back on the nuts-and-bolts realities of how the movie business worked. In my plodding, hardheaded Midwestern way, I tried my damnedest to figure out the puzzle and find a way in.

One of the things I learned was that, in almost all movie projects, the music is the last component to be added. The visuals are shot, the film is edited, *then* the music is dubbed in. Still, it's useful for the director to have at least a rough idea of how the eventual soundtrack will work, so film editors often use "temp music" when putting together a movie. They find a recording that *sort of* fits; if the director likes the feel of it, then the person who made the recording has the inside track at getting the gig to score the movie.

My first order of business, then, was to get a CD recorded and distributed. Fortunately for me, New Age music was surging in popularity at the time, and, broadly speaking, that was the idiom I was writing in. My first album, *The Waiting,* was released on Narada in 1987. I'm proud to say that it was critically well received and was at least modestly successful in the marketplace. But I could only hope that it was finding its way into the ears of film editors and moviemakers.

For better or worse, *The Waiting* turned out to be the perfect title for that album. I released it . . . and I waited. And I waited some more. Let me be clear that nothing happened quickly here!

Meanwhile, I started thinking about a second album. Everything being relative, a first album is easy. It uses up all the little scraps that have been stuck in drawers over the years, all the tunes and motifs that have been kicking around waiting to be explored and expanded. But a second album calls for fresh inspiration. And, for a number of difficult and dispiriting months, I didn't know where that inspiration would come from.

Then a close family friend gave me a book. It was *Son of the Morning Star*, by Evan S. Connell, and it absolutely captivated me. The narrative encompassed much of the history of the Plains Indians in late-nineteenth-century America. It told of their constant forced marches, the broken promises and ugly atrocities committed against them by a government intent on expansion at any cost. Reading that book, I was both moved and outraged. I also felt a nagging and surprisingly personal sense of loss. It wasn't only the Native Americans who had been displaced and deprived of much of their ancient culture; *all* of us had lost something when those Native traditions were trampled, when the old wisdom was scattered and devalued.

Inevitably, my strong reaction to *Son of the Morning Star* found its way into my work. I would not presume to say that I was writing Native American music; rather, I was trying in my own manner to understand and honor a certain tradition, to express my reverence and nostalgia for a way of life that had nearly been destroyed. These feelings largely shaped my second album, *One By One*, which was released in 1989.

Soon after this album was released—and *four years* after I'd first hatched my wish of writing for the movies—

I learned that Kevin Costner was making a film based on the life of the Plains Indians in the nineteenth century. Was this serendipity, or what? My album could hardly have been more on-message if I'd written it as an audition piece.

Through a rather tenuous connection from my Stanford days, I was able to get the recording to Costner. Kevin loved it and asked me to score the film. Just like that, my long-held wish was about to be fulfilled.

Or was it?

There was, it seemed, one small problem: I didn't actually know how to write a film score!

In retrospect, this is a real head-scratcher, but it happens to be true. In some ways, false modesty aside, I'd done a pretty savvy job of finessing my way toward the movie business. And yet I'd somehow managed to overlook the most basic requirement of all. Consumed by wishing, distracted by daydreams (and, in fairness to myself, busy with lots of other projects), I hadn't done the hard work of actually learning the craft. Somewhere along the line, I'd fallen into the trap of imagining that sheer desire would prepare me to seize my opportunity. Or that the perfect mentor would miraculously appear at the pivotal moment. Or that a studio head would see me as a diamond in the rough and just "take me as I am."

Surprise: None of that happened.

Too late, I started playing catch-up. I consulted with more experienced composers on orchestration. I gave myself a crash course in the technical side of moviemaking. But I knew, deep down, that I was ill-prepared, and the lack of self-assurance showed. In spite of myself, the message I sent was: This guy isn't ready.

Under other circumstances, I might perhaps have been able to persuade the studio that I was a quick study and they should take a chance on me. But there were complicating factors here. Aren't there always? Kevin Costner, while a well-established actor, was a first-time director; that made people nervous. The film he was planning, *Dances with Wolves*, was long, expensive, and thoroughly unconventional; that made people nervous, too. An unproven composer was apparently one too many things to be nervous about.

So I lost the gig but I learned a lesson. Two lessons, in fact.

The first one is about the nature of lucky breaks. I recorded an album inspired by the Plains Indians; Kevin Costner needed music for a film about the Plains Indians. What could be luckier than that?

But there's a big difference between a lucky break and a free pass. A lucky break seldom means that things are suddenly easy; rather, a lucky break often comes as an opportunity to rise to a challenge, to do something difficult. But you have to prove worthy of the lucky break by being ready to seize it.

This brings me to the second lesson, which is, of

course, about preparation. Could I have written an acceptable score for *Dances with Wolves*? I honestly believe I could have. But it would have involved a fair amount of learning on the fly, and that wasn't good enough. There's a subtle distinction, I believe, between being *capable* of doing something and being truly *prepared* to do it.

Meaningful preparation calls for a good deal of work in advance—confronting possible difficulties, thinking through potential pitfalls. This forethought, in turn, allows for clarity. Clarity is what allows us to demonstrate, both to ourselves and to those who might employ us, that we are truly up to the job at hand. That level of preparation is what earns true confidence.

My near-miss at getting to write the full score for *Dances with Wolves* did not turn out to be a total loss. Costner eventually asked me to compose a small piece called "Firedance"—a mere two minutes long, but, in my honest opinion, a pretty interesting rhythmic exercise and, more important, a thematic challenge as well. In those two minutes, I tried to capture and compress the essence of the story—to convey the mystery and excitement of a man transformed before our very eyes and ears. Coupled with great visuals and Costner's almost mystical intensity, the scene really clicked.

For me, then, getting to write "Firedance" was more than a consolation prize; it was a chance to demonstrate that I could, in fact, write effectively for the movies.

Writing *part* of a movie, rather than taking on responsibility for the whole grand sweep, was probably what was appropriate to my knowledge at the time. So, in that sense, I got my wish of writing for film, and the story has a happy ending.

Even so, I made a couple more mistakes in connection with "Firedance." Again, these were errors that came from my being inadequately prepared to face the realities of business and the requirements of my craft.

To the surprise of the skeptics, *Dances with Wolves* went on to become both a critical and popular success. A soundtrack album was a natural follow-up, but the main composer of the score, John Barry, did not want my music included in the playlist. In his view, it was his soundtrack, period; I more or less accepted that.

In retrospect, this was a blunder. It's not my way to raise my voice or stamp my feet, but there are professional and totally appropriate ways to fight for one's interests, and in this case I failed to do so. The stakes were real: meaningful exposure for my music. But I was not prepared to accept the harsh reality that sometimes even colleagues have to butt heads on matters of turf. I wanted to believe I was being a nice guy by not fighting to be included on the soundtrack; but in fact I was abdicating part of what it means to be a professional. I was more intent on avoiding conflict than in making the most of my work.

My other mistake with regard to "Firedance" had less

to do with the frictions of business and more to do with the demands of craft.

Since my piece was not included in the *Dances with Wolves* soundtrack, I was able to negotiate the right to put it on my third album, *Lost Frontier.* This was good. Instrumental music stations were playing my stuff; the success of the Costner film brought a wider audience to music with a Native American influence. But there was a fundamental problem with "Firedance." It was a two-minute piece, and two-minute pieces just didn't get played much on the radio.

I should have expanded it to a three- or four-minute song. But I didn't. Why not? I could play the purist card and say that the piece was meant to run two minutes, not three, end of story. But that kind of artistic stubbornness usually gets you nowhere, and can sometimes be a mask for a simple limitation of craft. The honest answer is that I didn't expand "Firedance" into a radio-friendly format because, at the time, I didn't know how. I just couldn't hear it.

Again, this suggests the distinction between ability and preparedness. If I'd been truly prepared for the opportunity to write "Firedance," I would have *anticipated* its possible success and the implications that went with it. I would have planned for its possible expansion or translation into other forms. I would have been ready to make more of it than in fact I did. But my wish had been to have my music in a feature film; I hadn't thought *beyond* that wish.

Which leads me to yet another dangerous thing about wishes.

Too often, I think, people see the fulfillment of a wish as a consummation, as the *end* of a process. But doesn't it make more sense to see a wish coming true as a beginning, as the start of something? The real excitement and the real fulfillment lie in seeing where that wish can lead.

Before leaving this issue of wishes and their dangers, let's turn the whole subject upside down and see how it looks from the opposite angle: What happens when wishes *aren't* granted?

Life may not be fair, but it often turns out to be surprisingly symmetrical, and I think an instance of that symmetry applies here. Consider: Just as the granting of a wish—as in the case of Midas—can sometimes prove to be a curse, the thwarting of a wish can sometimes end up being a hidden blessing.

In both instances, the same mechanism is at play: a confusion between what we *think* we want and what we *really* want. When a wish is denied—when we don't get what we *think* we want—we are forced to look farther afield, to think harder and more deeply about what we *really* want, what would truly make us happy. Sometimes a wish that doesn't come true is in fact a liberation.

Let me offer an example.

I know a young woman who comes from a family of lawyers. She was a serious and focused student, and, after a quite successful undergraduate career, she was accepted to one of the leading East Coast law schools. Wanting to make the most of the summer in between, she applied for an internship with a major New York corporate law firm.

She had good reason to believe that this was a fine way to jump-start a career. Her older sister had taken the same route, advancing from unpaid internships to paid ones, then to an associate's position on a clear track to partner. That first summer internship was a completely reasonable thing to wish for.

But she didn't get it. This was not her fault. Her academic credentials were as impressive as her sister's. I have no doubt that she gave every bit as good of an interview. But the world had changed. Business had slowed, law firms were contracting. With less work to go around, there was not much need for interns, and there were far fewer associate positions to dangle as eventual rewards. It was a clear case of life just not being fair.

The disappointment of her wish left the young woman understandably frustrated, angry, and, for a brief time, bewildered. A disappointed wish, after all, is a kind of small death; it calls for a letting-go, and letting go never comes easily or without some period of grieving and transition.

But there was still the question of how she'd spend her summer, and she didn't have the luxury of a lot of time to mope. She ended up taking a very modest-paying internship with a large environmental nonprofit on Long Island.

"I went in with a chip on my shoulder," she admits. "I felt like I was settling for a very distant second choice. The office work was totally routine. My bad attitude made it even worse. I just sort of refused to find it interesting."

Then something changed. The young woman was invited to accompany her more senior colleagues on their fieldwork, visiting wetlands and pine barrens and other environmentally fragile areas that her organization was working to protect.

"It was amazing," she recalls. "I was just so happy out there in my muddy boots. I felt energized, curious about everything, like a monkey let out of the cage. And I started thinking very hard about whether I wanted to spend my working life in a law office, under artificial light, wearing business suits and stockings, when I could be out here in khaki shorts and sunshine."

So what did this young woman decide to do? The story is still playing out. She's started law school as planned, though with a determination to focus on environmental, rather than corporate, matters. She says she might end up practicing law, working for the kind of nonprofit that would call for a certain amount of fieldwork; or she might jettison law altogether and segue into some branch of natural science. Stay tuned!

Whatever her eventual decision, however, the point is this: It was the denial of her first wish that allowed her to change course—to reevaluate her options and to discover a life that was more truly her own. If she'd gotten her first choice, why would she have deviated from what she *thought* she wanted?

Wishes steer us toward a certain longed-for destination; they tend to focus our attention on a particular pinpoint of a goal. And that's fine; having goals and reaching them can be a great source of self-respect and joy.

But there's a danger, too. A pinpoint goal can blind us to the universe of choices that exist in every imaginable direction. When a goal isn't reached—when a wish is denied—it forces us to rub our eyes and look again at a wider world.

10

What we mean when we say "success"

I think it's fair to say that we live in a society that is extremely preoccupied with the concept of "success."

We strive for success, we dream of success, we read books that promise surefire formulas for success. We praise, admire, and sometimes even fawn over the success of others. Sometimes we secretly, or not so secretly, envy and begrudge it as well. We seem to believe that success necessarily implies happiness and fulfillment, and that lack of success can breed only frustration and gloom.

But here's a question: For all our preoccupation with "success," how clear are we as to what we mean by the word?

In my own view, *success* should be defined with reference to the substance of a person's achievement. What is someone actually accomplishing? Is she helping others? Is he living up to his own unique potential? Is there passion and originality in her approach to life and work? Is there fundamental value in what he's trying to achieve?

Sadly, however, my impression is that *substance* has little to do with our concept of success these days. Rather than focusing on the essence of an enterprise or a career, we focus only on the *reward* it brings—generally as measured in dollars.

To put it another way, we seem to focus on the payoff rather than the process; and this misplacement of emphasis devalues the whole notion of what "success" really means. As it is commonly used, in fact, the word *successful* has become little more than a coded synonym for "well paid."

Think about it. In many social situations, it would be considered crass to speak of someone as "a surgeon who makes a lot of money" or "an executive who's paid a ton of dough." Generally speaking, though, when people refer to someone as "successful," isn't that what they're *really* saying?

Now, far be it from me to say that there's anything wrong with making money; that's not my point here at all. What I am saying, however, is that money should be seen as a spin-off of success, a side effect, and not the measure of success itself.

True success comes from within. It is a function of

who we are and what we do. It emerges from the mysterious chemistry of our abilities and passion and hard work and commitment. True success is something we earn privately and whose value we determine for ourselves.

The outside world can reward us with money, but it cannot anoint us with this deeper and more personal kind of success.

On the other hand, neither can the outside world *take away* the success that we've earned in our inmost hearts. And this has enormous implications of a very practical kind.

Anyone who's had his eyes open in recent years will have noticed that our economic system can be fickle, to say the least. A career that is rewarded one month is punished the next. An investment banker is showered with bonuses one year, then suddenly unemployed. An executive is seen as being on a fast track . . . until her firm goes belly-up.

What happens to the "success" those people enjoyed when things were going better? Does the success vanish as soon as the money spigot is turned off? If it can be undone so abruptly, how solid could it have been in the first place? Is it possible that maybe it was illusory all along?

If we were only talking about money here, these questions would not be so important. But in fact we're talking about the much more intimate and crucial things that are tied in with our definitions of success—things like self-respect and confidence and peace of mind.

If someone's self-respect is proportional to the size of her paycheck, what does she think of herself if the paycheck shrinks or disappears?

If someone's confidence is based on the next raise or the next promotion, how does he feel when his progress is stymied?

And why should any of us entrust the outside world, fickle and uncontrollable as it is, to tell us not just what our income will be, but what we are actually *worth*?

The bottom line, I believe, is that the blind acceptance of a money-based definition of success is just way too risky a proposition. Even leaving aside the intellectual and spiritual imperatives to find a more robust and personal definition of success and meaning, simple prudence should steer us away from measuring our worth by what others will pay us.

It is both lazy and dangerous to leave it to our bank statement to tell us how we're doing in our lives.

But, okay, if the passive acceptance of a money-based definition of success can lead to all sorts of dangers and blind alleys, how *should* we define success?

I don't believe that there's a one-size-fits-all answer to this question—and that's exactly the point.

A meaningful and resonant definition of success has to be *personal*. I can't define, still less dictate, what should constitute success for you; you can't define what should constitute success for me. Each of us must labor toward our own version of fulfillment.

Moreover, the work we do in the name of defining our success—work that brings us closer to self-knowledge and an understanding of what we truly value—becomes *part* of our success.

Let me try to make this clearer by way of an example.

I have a friend who is a wonderful person and a wonderful musician. He cares incredibly little about money or possessions—which is a good thing, as his music earns him only a modest and sporadic livelihood. He has positioned himself so far outside the economic mainstream that, at certain junctures, he has to spend time living in his car. Most people would regard this as an unenviable state of affairs, to say the least, and it's fair to say that this fellow has faced his share of challenges and frustrations. Still, he regards himself as a success in life, and I happen to totally agree with his assessment. He's living the life that is right for him; the life he has chosen for himself.

Finding that life—*creating* that life—was not easy. To do so, he had to confront his own ambivalence and insecurities. He had to come to terms with the expectations of others; and he had to accept the costs—both practical and emotional—of declining to meet those expectations.

His mother was a piano teacher, and he himself had shown great musical promise even as a child. His father was a loving but practical-minded man who wanted his son to grow up to become a doctor. The father worked hard and made sacrifices in the name of his child's education and future. Honoring his parents' commitment and their wishes, the young man decided that he would become a premed student, relegating his music to a side passion.

"In college," he recalls, "I recognized the love and respect between my dad and me. He saw all these possibilities for me. He wanted me to be successful and happy. So when I was studying premed, I didn't think, 'Dad, I'm doing this for you.' I really believed that the premed path was my own intent. I told myself I would pursue that path, and whatever came from that choice, that's what I would do."

By junior year of college, however, it was becoming clear that there was a problem. My friend's interest in medicine was waning; music was calling to him more insistently. When he broached the subject with his father, the conversation led to pain and confusion on both sides. "It's not like he was threatening to disown me," my friend recalls, "but still, it was clear that if I gave up medicine, our relationship would be changed and damaged. I couldn't expect the same kind of financial or emotional support. I'd really be on my own. The choice was mine to make."

And so began a long and convoluted struggle—a struggle that, I believe, is fairly typical of what happens when young people choose paths outside their parents' expectations. For a while longer, my friend tried his damnedest to fulfill his father's wishes, keeping up the premed curriculum and graduating with a degree in biochemistry. He wanted, after all, to be a good son. And it's also true that chasing his father's dream saved him from the anxiety of pursuing his own. Did he really know how to make himself a life in music? Was he ready to be a professional performer? Was he good enough? Would he *ever* be good enough?

Following his father's wishes spared him from having to answer these extremely daunting questions. In some ways, it's easier to settle for someone else's version of success than to risk falling short at one's own.

Still, life has many ways of asserting itself—and they aren't always very direct. At some point, my friend, probably unconsciously, found himself erecting roadblocks against his chances of becoming a doctor. He applied only to the most difficult programs at the most selective med schools. He worked hard at his studies and his applications—and at the very same time, he resisted the direction in which those efforts were taking him. A soft but steady inner voice, what Socrates called his *daemon* and what my friend refers to as his design, was telling him ever more insistently that he should be going somewhere else.

Eventually, inevitably, my friend quit the doctor path

and made music the center of his life. His mother was supportive of this. With the father, unfortunately, there was a rift—not an angry break, but a distance that carried with it a note of mutual guilt and disappointment.

"I had to accept that and acknowledge it," says my friend. "And then I had to let it go. Over time, I tried to see what was positive in it. My father's aspirations for me—what were they based on in the first place? They were based on love and on a faith in my abilities—his belief that I had something to give to the world. So okay, I haven't taken the path he would have chosen for me. But still, I can justify his faith in me by what I accomplish on my own path."

This story has a lovely kicker.

Not long ago—thirty years after his difficult choice to abandon medicine!—my friend was giving a musical performance. Afterward, he was approached by an audience member, a practicing physician, who told him how uplifted he'd been by the concert. The doctor called my friend a healer.

"At last," says my friend, "someone had—with a few simple words—pulled together what my father wanted for me and what I'd chosen for myself. What a liberation!"

I'd like to add a brief and very personal coda to this story, because I have had my own experience with the liberating power of a few simple words.

Sometime in my twenties, by which time I'd answered the call of music but was making only a modest living at it, I was visiting family in Omaha. I'd had some conversations with my father, in the course of which I had tried to explain my ambitions, my goals, and my plans for reaching them. In truth, I was using these conversations, in part, to explain things to *myself*; I was asking my father to be a sort of correcting mirror that could gather somewhat scattered shards of thought and reflect back clarity.

As was his custom, my father listened carefully, without judging, without offering explicit advice. Then one day, almost in passing as he was headed out the door, he said to me, "You know, Pete, you and I really do the same thing. Music is your canvas. Berkshire's my canvas and I get to paint a little every day."

That was all he said—and it was plenty.

It was a validation that I needed then and cherish even now. My father, as successful as he was, was comparing what he did to what I did. And not only comparing them, but in some sense equating them—not, of course, in terms of economic potential or impact in the wider world, but in terms of fundamental, *personal* legitimacy.

We didn't have to define *success* in the same way. We didn't have to adopt the same criteria for "keeping score." What mattered was our shared process, not the rewards we netted. What mattered was that we were both following our respective passions.

What connected us was that we were both trying our best at lives we'd chosen for ourselves. My father's acknowledgment of this was a tremendous gift to me.

The preceding stories suggest, I think, a basic paradox about our definitions of success: The truest and most durable measures of success are the ones we choose and define *for ourselves,* but those choices and definitions don't happen in a vacuum. Even our most personal choices and values are shaped, in part, by influences outside our skin.

Family expectations, of course, constitute one such set of influences. This is inevitable and also fitting. Parents, after all, have seen more of life than kids have. They want the best for their sons and daughters, and they have their own considered ideas about what "the best" consists of. Sometimes the kids happily accept the parents' version of success; sometimes they reject it.

But the point I'd like to make is this: A son may conform or rebel; a daughter may adopt her parents' dreams or veer off in a quite different direction toward her own. Either way, their choices will be made *with reference to* their family's expectations. This could not be otherwise; it's human nature. Even—or maybe especially!—when we decide to flout our families' expectations, we have to acknowledge that the power of those expectations is legitimate and real.

As it is with family expectations, so it is with peer pressure and social fashion. But when it comes to definitions of success, fashion is fickle, just like it is in regard to hemlines or lapel width.

There is no one version of "success" that has been agreed upon and esteemed in all places and at all times. In Periclean Athens, success meant having time and leisure to hang out and talk with the philosophers. Among certain monastic orders, success means letting go of all attachments and desires, breaking off dependence on the material world: having nothing and needing nothing. But success can also be counted in goats or grandchildren. Sometimes "honor"—however defined—is esteemed far above wealth; in other times and places, wealth seems to count above all else.

Given all these varied definitions of success, it should be clear that *success*, in fact, is a very peculiar kind of noun! T[illegible] about it: We can all pretty much agree, for example, on [illegible] hair is. Say "tree" or "book" or "steering wheel," and most of us will picture something real and solid—something whose existence does not depend on our opinion. Does *success* even exist in that same way?

Success, basically, is whatever we decide to call success.

If this is circular, I think it should also be liberating. Why should people be captives to something that doesn't even exist, except by a consensus that is always shifting?

• • •

But for all of that, people are shaped by the times and the societies they live in, and there's no denying the power of social fashion. As with family expectations, an era's dominant version of success is something we can accept or fight against. What we *can't* do is pretend it isn't there or that it isn't, at some level, a factor in the choices that we make.

Signing on with a dominant version of success is relatively easy. This is not to say that *achieving* success is easy; it almost never is. But *aiming* for the species of success that's in style at a given moment is pretty simple. It requires no great originality or soul-searching. It's mainly a matter of going with the momentary flow, subscribing to the same set of criteria and priorities that *most* people have agreed to honor.

By contrast, adopting a personal version of success that's at variance with the fashionable kind takes a fair amount of thought and strength of character. And this is true no matter what the dominant version of success happens to be. Back around 1969, say, it would have taken real imagination and courage for a young person to say, "You know what? I think I'd really like to be a stockbroker!"

In more recent decades, of course, our consensual definition of success seems to have become more and more narrowly involved with money, pure and simple.

Everything *except* earning power has become relatively devalued.

This trend kicked in during the 1980s, a decade when business school applications reached historic highs and *Time* magazine was doing cover stories about the rise of Yuppiedom. A friend of mine recently passed along a rather horrifying anecdote that neatly sums up the dominant ethos of that time.

"I was at a party," he recalled, "and the host introduced me to a woman friend of his. She asked me what I did—which was generally the first thing people wanted to know about each other back then. I told her I was a writer. She looked me up and down—shoes to haircut—and said exactly one word: 'Successful?'

"The question struck me as so rude and crass that, for a moment, I couldn't even speak. This person had zero interest in what I actually did. What did I write about? What drove me to write? Was my stuff funny? Tragic? It was all the same to her if I wrote limericks or if I'd just completed a massive treatise that explained the meaning of life. All that mattered was whether I was making a lot of dough. I finally managed to mumble, 'I get by,' and I moved off toward the bar."

If that sort of narrow and even obsessive emphasis on money led to nothing worse than rude remarks at parties, I suppose it wouldn't matter very much. But, in fact, defining success in terms of reward rather than the actual *content* of one's work has an array of very real and serious consequences.

Perhaps the most important consequence is this: Our definition of success at a given time has a way of funneling people toward certain professions—and funneling them *away from* others. If money is the sole criterion by which we separate the "winners" from the "losers," then people will tend to go where the money is.

Or where it *seems* to be.

That, however, can lead to problems of a very practical sort. Back in the 1980s, the hot career was management consulting; so many people chased that particular Grail that, not surprisingly, there soon came to be a glut of management consultants. Fashion swung to lawyering . . . until there were too many lawyers. More recently, the tide turned toward investment banking, and we've seen where that particular fixation got us. The point is that, even if we follow a rainbow whose only color is money green, there's just no guarantee that there'll be a pot of gold at the end.

But okay, that's just the *economic* risk of a version of success that revolves around money. What about the emotional and spiritual and social risks?

What about the callings that don't get answered because they are unlikely to lead to wealth?

What about the curiosity and creativity that go unfulfilled because they are seen as dangerous distractions from the pursuit of money?

What about the professions built on *content*, not reward?

Consider teaching as a prime example. There is no more important profession. No profession touches more lives; no profession has a bigger influence in shaping both individual and collective futures. Moreover, teachers must bring *all* of themselves to the job—heart as well as mind, sheer physical energy as well as expertise.

In terms of content, teaching is *huge*. In terms of monetary reward, it is not. And this means that, when money tops our list of priorities, there are many talented people who won't even consider a career in teaching.

Clearly, whenever someone who might make a great teacher decides not to be one, it's a loss for kids. But there's another side to this as well: It's a potentially even bigger loss to the person who shuns the classroom for some better-paying workplace.

What are the satisfactions he's missing out on, in favor of a bigger paycheck? What opportunities for personal growth is she trading for a signing bonus? At the end of the day, will these people feel better about serving a corporation or about helping children learn?

Again, adopting a version of success that is out of fashion at a given time requires courage and imagination—a determination to decide for oneself what really matters. There are professions more likely to make us rich in terms of money; there are professions more likely to make us rich in terms of spirit. If these latter professions are to flourish, we need to invest them with a kind of respect and prestige that can't be counted in dollars. We have to be reminded of how *intrinsically* valuable they are.

Fortunately, there are at least some people who are working at doing exactly that. One of them is a man named Taylor Mali, a poet and teacher who has taken it as his mission to enlarge upon the dignity of teaching. I recently came across a poem of his, in which he describes a dinner party attended by members of various professions. Inevitably, at some point the conversation turns to earnings, and an attorney in the gathering asks the teacher what he makes. Mali brilliantly turns the question upside down, as this excerpt will attest. (The entire poem can be found at www.taylormali.com.)

You want to know what I make?
I make kids work harder than they ever thought they could . . .
I make parents see their children for who they are and what they can be . . .
I make kids wonder,
I make them question.
I make them criticize.
I make them apologize and mean it.
I make them write, write, write.

And then I make them read.
You want to know what I make?
I make a goddamn difference! What about you?

Years ago, in a book about Zen Buddhism, I came across a quote that has stayed with me all this time, because it is the sort of mysterious and elusive pronouncement that seems to hint at a meaning far beyond the simple words: *The key to the treasure is the treasure.*

I mention this here because I believe it has application to our notions about success.

Consider: It seems to be a habit of mind to imagine "success" as a literal thing—a pirate chest, say, full of gold or jewels or whatever it is we decide to value. But what good is a treasure chest if we can't open it?

And how can we open it if the key we hold in our hand is not a match to the particular treasure chest we're trying to open?

This, I think, is the sense in which the key to the treasure *is* the treasure. There are any number of possible treasures out there waiting to be claimed, but it is the key that each of us holds in our hand that determines which one might be ours.

And this mysterious key that each of us possesses—what is it made of? It's made of our own unique mix of talents, inclinations, and passions. The treasure that can be unlocked by that key, and by that key only, is the version of success we define for ourselves.

Life is what we make it, and part of succeeding lies in breaking through to a clear understanding of what our own success should look like. No one else can tell us how to measure or describe it. No one else can judge whether we've reached our goals or fallen short.

The world can throw rewards at us, or can withhold them. That's the world's business. But the world can't judge the fundamental value and legitimacy of what we are trying to achieve. That's *our* business. The success we define for ourselves is the treasure that cannot be tarnished or taken away.

11

The perils of prosperity

It is a central belief of mine that people are more alike than different.

Beyond the happenstance of things like birthplace and skin color and material circumstances, we share a common set of hopes and fears, needs and longings. We can all experience the joy of love and friendship. None of us is a stranger to the pain of conflict and loss. We mostly agree on what is funny and what is sad. We are all fellow travelers in the search for meaning.

Why do the great stories and the great mythologies ring true in all times and places? Because—as we have seen in the Midas story, for example—they address and shed light on the feelings and yearnings that are common to us all.

Why is music regarded as the universal language? Because it does not depend on the varying words we use to describe things; rather, it cuts straight to the emotions and the energy that exist within each of us, and that words can only approximately describe.

In these pages, I have tried my best to celebrate our shared humanity by talking about things I believe to be universal: the need for solid values; the challenge of finding and answering our own vocations; the importance of acknowledging and learning from our mistakes, and of deciding for ourselves what the concept of success is really all about.

Those issues, I believe, apply to all of us. But it's also true that they will play out differently in different lives. In this regard, variables like place of birth and material circumstances do matter. While, at the end of the day, the American prep school student and the West African villager have the same yearnings for security, self-respect, and peace of mind, the particular routes they take to get there, and the exact challenges along the way, will probably be very different.

In this chapter, then, I would like to return in greater detail to a subject I've only touched on so far—namely, the specific risks and pitfalls facing affluent families as they try to pass along good values to their kids.

Clearly, all families *want* to pass along good values. I've never yet met a father who wanted his child to grow up spoiled or lazy; I've never yet met a mother who wanted her kids to be greedy or smug. The problem, though, is that there is sometimes a great distance between the message that's intended and the message that's actually conveyed. The reasons for this are complicated and bedeviling—part of why there's no such thing as being a *perfect* parent.

I once heard a story that vividly illustrates how these intended messages sometimes get garbled and how the best intentions sometimes backfire.

There was a man who had grown up in a family of modest means, but one with a great work ethic and a high regard for education. His parents sacrificed to put him through college; he himself took on part-time jobs as well as student loans—loans that became a serious burden when he decided to go on to medical school.

But he ended up with dual degrees in medicine and engineering. Using his quite rare combination of skills and expertise, he went on to design a device that allowed seriously ill patients to dispense their own pain medication in safe and limited doses. He patented the device, which he then licensed to a major pharmaceutical company for a hefty sum as well as ongoing royalties.

Quite suddenly he was a wealthy man.

By the time his own children came along, he'd been wealthy for some years. By then, it was a given that the family lived in a big house in a nice neighborhood, that Mom and Dad both drove shiny new cars, that they could eat in fancy restaurants and take winter vacations in places where the sun was always shining.

The father, of course, was happy to provide a comfortable and privileged life for his children. But he was also concerned that they were getting a skewed and very partial view of what life was really all about.

He'd seen the whole progression of stages and challenges that had eventually made him wealthy. He remembered the hard work, the sacrifices, the pressure and anxiety of indebtedness. He remembered that it was his own less than prosperous parents who had instilled in him the confidence and motivation to make his mark in the world. He remembered, too, that in designing his pain-relief mechanism, he hadn't just been trying to make a lot of money; he'd been trying to help people and to make a meaningful contribution to how medicine was practiced.

The kids had seen none of this firsthand. This was not their fault, nor was it his; they just came along at a different part of the curve. Still, it left the father with a dilemma. He was not the sort of person who bragged of his accomplishments. He certainly didn't want to make his kids feel guilty about their advantages.

At the same time, he *did* want them to understand that wealth and material comfort did not come about by magic or because their family was somehow more deserving than others; these things were the result of effort. He wanted his children, as well, to understand the difference between wealth and fundamental human worthiness; they were no better than people who had less; they were not inferior to people who had more.

The summer his oldest son turned sixteen, the father came up with a stratagem for exposing the boy to some of these basic life lessons. The family belonged to a country club—one of those old-line places where members still walked the golf course while caddies carried the bags. It was decided that the son would caddy for the summer. Caddying was good, healthy, outdoor work; it was also difficult and selfless. It entailed taking on the drudgery while other people had the fun. It demanded remaining cheerful and polite if one hoped to make good tips. Moreover, the boy would be working alongside grown men who'd been caddies for many years and who would always be caddies; the father hoped that his son would feel a solidarity with these men, a respect for their knowledge, a recognition that there was dignity in their exhausting and modest-paying work.

So the boy carried other people's golf bags for a couple months, and at the end of the summer the father asked him what he'd learned from the experience.

"I learned," said the son, "that I better make a lot of money, so I can have other people carry the bags for *me*."

That was the takeaway? The father was understandably baffled and chagrined. This was quite the opposite of the lesson he had hoped his son would learn. What about an honest regard for hard physical work? What about compassion for the people whose entire working lives would consist of that kind of labor? Why hadn't the son absorbed *those* messages?

The father had no idea—and truthfully, who can say? Maybe the members whose golf bags he'd carried had put ideas in his head that contravened his father's hopes for the experience. Maybe the other caddies just weren't very nice to him.

Or maybe, for better or worse, the son's basic character and values had already been shaped by a complex web of people and events—by all the mysterious influences and unexamined assumptions that might go with growing up wealthy, but with an insufficient understanding of how the wealth had come to be.

Could the father, possibly, have done a better job—not just during one adolescent summer, but through the son's whole upbringing—of explaining how the family's prosperity had come about? Could he have more clearly conveyed the satisfaction that came from starting with very little, and succeeding on one's own merits? Could he have made it clearer that the essence of success lay in focused effort and the substance of an accomplishment, and not in the reward that sometimes resulted? Was the caddying experiment just too little too late?

Probably no one but the father himself could answer

these questions. But I do think they're the kind of questions that need to be addressed when we think about the subtle and many-sided job of passing on good values.

In the foregoing anecdote, the son heard a message very different from the one the father thought he was sending, and the unintended result was to focus the young man's ambition solely on making money so that he could maintain his privileged lifestyle. The father was disappointed in this . . . but at least the kid had *some* species of ambition!

For some wealthy families, the problem is that ambition seems to be lacking in their sons and daughters. Why work hard if one's economic future already seems secure? Why strive, if striving only brings you more of what you already have? What's left to do if Mom or Dad or some more distant forebear has already made a mark in the world and established the family's prominence?

These are understandable sentiments; but they are also dangerous and subversive. They can suck the joy and the juice right out of life. So let's try to address them here and now.

Why work hard? Because it's the surest and possibly the only route to self-respect.

Why strive? Because striving brings out the best in us;

it tells us who we are, what we have to offer, how much we're capable of achieving.

What's left to do after the family's prosperity has been established? *Everything!*

This last point, I think, should be obvious—making money, after all, constitutes just one small part of the whole range of human activities and possibilities. Still, our society puts such a heavy emphasis on earning a living, that other goals and aspirations are sometimes overshadowed.

The great majority of people work because they have to. Food costs money! There is rent or a mortgage to be paid. These are bedrock economic realities, and there is dignity and justified pride in meeting their challenges.

But when money ceases to be the primary motivator, there are *other* challenges that are equally compelling and equally legitimate.

Or are they?

Bear with me on this, because I think there's an important distinction to be made here.

I absolutely believe that other challenges and other ambitions—things like creative fulfillment or public service—are every bit as valid as ambitions geared toward money. But it doesn't matter what *I* say; it matters what *you* believe in your heart of hearts. And for some sons and daughters of wealthy parents, this becomes a real stumbling block. Having money—"coming from" money, as the saying goes—is so much a part of how they define themselves and their place in the world, that it takes a real leap of imagination and courage to embrace other parts of life as equally legitimate and equally defining.

Consider the example of a woman I've met, the daughter of a family that had amassed considerable wealth in the retailing field. As an adolescent, she had little interest in commerce. Still, she dutifully studied business administration in college and went on to get an M.B.A. That, for her, was default mode—the path that best fit her family's place in the world . . . but not necessarily her own.

Her own passion was for drawing and painting. She'd loved the art classes she'd taken as a little girl; whenever possible, she took studio courses all through college. She believed she had some talent; but at the same time, she had trouble taking her artistic inclinations seriously. What did making sketches have to do with the *real* business of life—or at least the real business of life as it was lived by her family, i.e., making money? Was she anything more than a dabbler?

She wrestled with these questions for a number of unhappy years, while working listlessly in the family business. As she described it later, she felt like she was sleepwalking through life, going through the motions without ever being truly engaged. She still painted, but she chafed at the thought that painting was her *hobby*. Not that there's anything wrong with having hobbies . . . but when a certain activity feels really *central* to one's life, calling it a hobby—and having it regarded by others as a hobby—is more than a little frustrating.

The frustration finally became unbearable, and the young woman worked up the courage to tell her parents she was leaving the family business to work full-time as an artist.

"I felt the strangest mix of emotions," she recalls. "I was tremendously relieved. I was excited and energized. And in some deep-down way, I felt like a failure. I don't think my parents put that on me. I think I put it on myself. I felt like I was punting on the so-called serious side of life, to indulge myself in being a bohemian. The funny part was that I think my father sort of liked being able to brag about *my artist daughter with the loft downtown*. Our family could afford an eccentric or two, so what was the harm? The only problem was whether I myself could believe that the life I was choosing would count for anything."

This, I thought, was an interesting choice of words. Count? Count *how*? In dollars? Could you count beauty? Could you count personal expression? Again, the hurdle this woman was facing was truly believing in the validity of her own ambition—an ambition that was not centered on earning power.

Eventually she made her peace with the choice she'd made. How did she persuade herself that her path was a legitimate one and that her ambition was serious? *By taking it very seriously herself.*

"At some point," she recalls, "I had a breakthrough. I realized that the measure of my legitimacy was not *what* I did but *how* I did it. If I was lazy or complacent about my painting, then I was just one more dabbler with a trust fund. Where was the self-respect in that? But if I worked hard, if I poured my heart and soul into the canvasses and kept trying to expand the boundaries of what I could do, then I was justified in calling myself an artist. The rest didn't matter. Did the world think I was great? Who cared? Was I ever going to make a lot of money doing this? Maybe, maybe not. I just had to reeducate myself so that I understood that there were plenty of honorable ambitions beyond the set that I'd grown up with."

Let me return, in this connection, to my own family and my own experience.

As I've mentioned, we weren't rich when I was growing up. We were certainly comfortable, but in a decidedly un-showy Midwestern way. My parents drove sensible cars that they kept for many years; my siblings and I were dressed in durable clothes without designer labels. As kids, we didn't take anything for granted. I received a small allowance, but it wasn't simply handed to me; I earned it by doing little chores around the house. If I borrowed a couple dollars to go downtown, I was expected to bring back change.

Over time, my parents started growing wealthy, and I was incredibly fortunate to witness something whose value and importance I have come only gradually to appreciate, and for which I am endlessly grateful to my parents.

What I witnessed was this: Even though our circumstances changed, my mother and father never did.

My mother was still the warm and giving person who had friends in every part of town and who cared so much about other people's stories.

My father still worked six days a week, wearing his trance-like concentration along with his khaki pants and cardigans.

Why didn't the money change them? Because making lots of money had never been the object of the exercise. My father worked extremely hard because he loved what he did, because it challenged and excited him. Money came eventually, but the passion and the curiosity were there from the start. Money followed; it never led.

I can't stress enough the importance of this distinction. In terms of the often wordless lessons that daughters and sons absorb, it is absolutely crucial.

If parents love their work and approach it with passion, then kids will come to see the value of *work itself,* and will be inclined to seek and discover a passion of their own.

If parents *don't* love and respect their work, but see it only as a necessary evil on the road to wealth and status, then the kids will absorb that lesson, too. It's a lesson that tends to lead to a lot of frustration and unhappiness in later life.

I recently heard about a family whose story provides a sad but vivid example of this.

The father was a quite successful investment banker. Now, I'm sure there are many people who genuinely enjoy the intellectual challenges and high-stakes action of investment banking, but this man wasn't one of them. By his own acknowledgment, he hated his job, and he spent every day of a twenty-five-year career looking forward to retirement.

Although he loathed his work, he was good at it, and he made a lot of money. But this set in motion a perverse logic that carried over to the next generation.

The process went something like this: Because the father detested his job, he felt he should somehow *pay himself back* for the unhappiness he felt at the office. And the only payback available was money, which therefore became way too important to him. Wanting to make even *more* money, he worked still harder at the job he hated, thereby adding to his unhappiness. And meanwhile, the perks of wealth accumulated—the summer house, the extravagant vacations, the memberships at fancy clubs.

But there was a problem even with the perks. The

father couldn't truly enjoy them, because he was looking to them for more than they could in fact provide. He wasn't seeking mere creature comforts or even luxury; he was looking to the rewards of wealth to fill a hole in his psyche. He was asking *stuff* to stand in for fulfillment. And that just doesn't work.

Now cut to the next generation.

The family had a son who, like most sons, admired his father and had a youthful, and largely unexamined, impulse to emulate him. When the time came for the young man to settle into a career, he made a different choice—he went into real estate development—but still, certain patterns were being unconsciously repeated. And they weren't healthy patterns. It took the younger man years of unhappiness and hundreds of hours of therapy to finally see these patterns clearly and break out of their thrall.

"I never liked my work," he recalls. "But for a while that didn't bother me much, because I didn't realize that a person *could* like his work! I just didn't know it was possible. What I'd seen at home was my father grinding it out, drinking Scotch, taking aspirin, and getting rich. I thought that was the deal."

Eventually, though, that deal came to seem unacceptable. The young man, like his father, proved to be good at what he did. The money came—and it left him feeling empty. "I was in a classic double bind," he says. "If I continued as I was, I saw nothing but misery up ahead. And if I *didn't* continue, I'd feel like a failure—less of a man than my father was."

At that point he decided to go into therapy.

"I learned a lot of things in therapy," he recalls, "but maybe the central one was this: I realized that what I'd absorbed from my father wasn't really a work ethic. It was a *suffering* ethic. Dad had suffered on the job, presumably for the good of the family. Therefore, I should suffer, too. If I didn't, I was shirking. Work was *supposed* to be painful. How could I have learned anything different?"

The powerful but unhappy example of his father, then, was controlling his life. Yet the son had an advantage that the father *hadn't* had: He'd had the opportunity to witness, from an early age, the futility of imagining that money alone could ever provide contentment. He *knew*, at some level, that his father's path, and his own, was not a road that led to true satisfaction or peace of mind. Rather, it was a road that led to success in the eyes of the world, but atrophy in one's own heart and soul.

Still, the values, good or bad, absorbed in childhood are the hardest things to unlearn, and doubting the wisdom of his own path was not the same thing as having the will and courage to step off it and start over. *That* took more time, lots of soul-searching, and the risk of conflict with his parents—who, understandably, would see the son's new direction as an implied reproach.

But each of us has both the great challenge and the

tremendous opportunity of crafting the life that's right for us. At some point, the young man drew the line and decided that building a life around work he disliked was just plain pointless. He extricated himself from his business commitments and decided to go back to school.

"I was past thirty by then," he recalls, "and I finally got around to thinking about what I actually *wanted* to do. Forget the paycheck or the prestige pecking order. What really *grabbed* me? What I came up with was counseling. I thought about how much I'd benefited from my own therapy. It might be overly dramatic to say that good counseling saved my life, but it certainly *steered* my life in a really helpful way. I wanted to do that for other people, to pass it along.

"So now that's what I do. I make a decent living, neither more nor less. But I love my work—and I don't feel guilty about loving it! I get up in the morning knowing that I'm going to learn something that day, and hopefully help somebody else. I've learned something precious that I could never have learned at home: that the work should be its own reward."

All parents want a good life for their kids. And the great majority of families, even families that are already prosperous, imagine that there's some even better life that they can pass along to their daughters and their sons.

These are truisms, clichés. We accept them without much thought or hesitation. But maybe we shouldn't. Maybe we should think a little harder about these simple words and basic concepts.

How confident are we—how confident *should* we be?—about our notions of what a good life actually *is*? What do we mean when we talk about a "better" life? Does it just equate with more money and more stuff? Do we even think about what might be lost while money and material comforts are being gained?

In early 2009, on a trip to Abu Dhabi, the capital of the United Arab Emirates, I was led to a fresh perspective on these very basic questions. Like the other Persian Gulf states, the U.A.E. is a nation to which modernization has come with dizzying speed; it is also a place where the wealthy live at a level of opulence that is almost inconceivable even to prosperous Westerners. In terms of what is gained and lost when "progress" and money displace tradition and self-reliance, Abu Dhabi presented a set of issues not so very different from those faced in our own society—but made more vivid and dramatic by their extremity and their compression in time.

One day I was privileged to be the lunch guest of a very high-ranking sheikh. He was a worldly and sophisticated man, but also someone who had remained connected with his Bedouin roots. His "compound" was luxurious, but modeled, broadly speaking, on a nomad's camp, with round buildings resembling tents. He had also retained the Bedouin's insistence on the importance of hospitality; in the desert, after all, travelers perished if they weren't offered food and shelter. Here in metro Abu Dhabi, there wasn't too much chance of starving; still, the sheikh made a point of inviting foreign visitors to dine with him. I later learned that he invited thirty or forty people to *every* lunch and *every* dinner, and fed them lavishly on camel meat and other local delicacies.

The food was presented by servants; the sheikh himself plated it, by hand. Other servants flanked the banquet hall, holding machine guns. There was a certain level of danger, after all, in so much conspicuous luxury.

In spite of his remarkable wealth, the sheikh was a humble man who spoke freely about his own modest beginnings. When he was a child, there'd been no plumbing and no electricity. There had been no schools—or at least no school buildings. Children sat under a tree with a teacher. There was a stick placed in the ground; when the stick's shadow reached a certain point, the school day was over. The Koran was the only book, and as such, it was not only a religious document, but also a reading primer; there was no other way to learn to read. As for food, people ate what the harsh land provided. Foreign goods were all but unheard of.

I remarked on the amazing changes the sheikh had seen in the course of his lifetime, and suggested that the young people of his country were so much better off today.

My host was not so sure. "They won't starve," he said. "They won't die of thirst. But I worry about our young. Many of them don't know who they are, or how the world they live in came to be. They go to American schools. They drive German cars. They wear designer clothes from France. All very nice—but what does it have to do with *them?*"

The privileged young, he felt, were being estranged from their own lives. So much had been handed to them that their own ambitions hardly seemed to matter, and since they didn't seem to matter much, those ambitions dwindled. Many young people loitered, both physically and spiritually, because there was no particular place they needed to be. Most of the young, the sheikh believed, were good and caring people who would do worthwhile things if they only knew how, but their lives had not prepared them for worthwhile things, and so their potential went untapped.

History had moved so fast in their part of the world that the customs of even one generation earlier seemed archaic and incomprehensible; how much connection could an urban, secular young man in a Porsche and Ray-Bans feel for his father, sitting under a date palm in the desert, reading the Koran?

Listening to the sheikh, I realized that his concerns for

the future of his own society applied to ours as well. The danger was a sad and life-diminishing alienation—people not really knowing where they are because they haven't taken the time to notice how they got there. People mistaking fleeting pleasure for durable joy, the emblems of status for genuine accomplishment.

These were symptoms that went with loss of meaning; *connection* was perhaps the only way to heal them. This did not mean a turning back or a blind acceptance of old beliefs; but it *did* mean a respect and understanding of the old ideals that had set the stage for the new prosperity.

It meant connection to the fundamental truths that had existed before the money appeared and would still be true after the money was gone.

It required connection, most basically of all, to one's own life—to the thoughts and yearnings and ambitions that come from within, that have a value that cannot be counted in dollars and cannot be *devalued* by preexisting wealth.

12

The gentle art of giving back

Whatever your religious inclinations—or the absence of them—it's hard to deny that there is some magnificent poetry in the book of Ecclesiastes. Consider this passage (first borrowed by Pete Seeger as a lyric for his song "Turn! Turn! Turn!," which was later turned into a 1960s hit by the Byrds):

> *To every thing there is a season, and a time to every purpose under heaven.*
> *A time to be born, and a time to die; a time to plant, and a time to pluck up that which is planted . . .*
> *A time to get, and a time to lose; a time to keep, and a time to cast away . . .*

As I read it, this "casting away" is really what, in more modern parlance, we would refer to as "giving back." It follows the phases of "getting" and "keeping." It is a stage of life when we have gathered many good things—experience, knowledge, and compassion, as well as material wealth—and we begin to feel the rightness, even the necessity, of sharing what the world has given us, of dispersing it for the good of others.

For most of this book, I've been talking about earlier stages of our individual journeys—I don't necessarily mean earlier in chronological terms, but in terms of our own development. How our most basic values are formed and passed along. The process of finding our bliss and developing the courage to answer our vocations. The painful but redemptive experience of learning from our mistakes. The challenge, both intellectual and emotional, of defining a version of success that resonates not just in society but *within* us.

Each of these steps, I believe, is crucially important in our personal growth. But there remains a further question: Where is the development *heading*? What is it *for*?

I think there are two sets of answers to these questions. The answers are complementary; there is no conflict between them.

At the level of the individual, our development is aimed at the self-respect that can come only from earning our own rewards. Our goal is the peace of mind that derives from choosing our own lives, pursuing the destiny that feels truly like our own.

At the level of society, our most meaningful progress is that which brings us to a point of being able to give back.

This giving back can take a million different forms. It resides equally in the grandest gestures and the smallest kindnesses. Teaching and mentoring are ways of giving back. Donating time is at least as important as donating money. Directing our work *outward,* toward the common good, rather than for private gain, is a way of giving back. Stretching beyond our comfort zone to engage a wider world is a way of giving back.

When the giving back involves significant sums of money, we seem to feel the need to attach a fancier word to it. We call it *philanthropy.*

But this, in my view, is another instance of a familiar word being sloppily used, and therefore straying from its original—and purer—meaning. As commonly used, philanthropy seems to apply *only* to large cash contributions, as if giving back were the sole prerogative of the wealthy and the socially prominent.

In its original definition, however, *philanthropy* has nothing to do with money or status. The word derives from two Greek roots: *philo-,* which means "love," and also, of course, yields the word *philosophy,* or love of knowledge; and *anthropos,* or "humankind," as in *anthropology.* With the cobwebs dusted off, then, we see that *philanthropy* means nothing more or less than the expression of the love we feel for one another, the sense of solidarity that makes us want to share.

Money can help; of course it can. But it is not the essence of philanthropy. The essence is the spirit in which the giving back is practiced. And developing that spirit is within the reach of all of us.

Some people seem to believe that giving back is basically just an "add-on" to a successful life. We've made money; we give some of it away again. The giving becomes a token of our standing; the more we donate, the more important we must be. And of course the sharing of our wealth can help to relieve that pernicious sense of "gift guilt"—the discomfort that goes with being among the lucky ones in an unfair world.

There is nothing wrong with any of that. The impulse to give is always a positive. Charitable donations are always welcome!

But I would argue that the most genuine and consequential forms of giving back are much more than an add-on. Rather, they are an integral part of who we are and what we do; they spring organically from our values and beliefs. Unlike, say, the mere writing of a check, this more personal sort of giving back is not a one-way transaction. It's the beginning of what I think of as an *enrichment loop*.

We give of ourselves; we get back from the world; we discover that we have yet more to give.

I'm happy to say that I can illustrate the workings of this loop with an example from my own experience.

As I've mentioned, fairly early in my career I started growing restless with what had been my bread-and-butter work, writing music for commercials. So I segued into writing songs and producing my own CDs. This was relatively more fulfilling, but still left me with a nagging question: What was the music *for*? I'd been blessed with at least a certain degree of talent and the wherewithal to follow my own passion; wasn't there some larger purpose or meaning toward which my efforts should be geared?

At around this time, I became captivated—by which I mean not only intellectually curious, but emotionally touched as well—by Native American culture and history. And this, as I realized only in retrospect, was the beginning of a wonderful enrichment loop.

Like any person of conscience, I was ashamed and horrified at the treatment meted out to the Indians by the white government and settlers and the idea of "manifest destiny." In the name of "progress," Native people had been lied to, double-crossed, and massacred. The land they lived on had been taken away and subjected to a concept of "ownership" that was completely foreign to their society. Much more than mere acreage was lost along the way. Native cultures—the product of thousands of years of observation, knowledge, and living sustainably with nature—had been trampled and dismissed. Who could imagine the value of the wisdom—environmental, spiritual, social, even medical—that had been so disrespectfully swept aside?

I resolved to do something to call attention to the importance of indigenous knowledge, and to help foster a climate of interest and respect in which at least some fragments of Native beliefs and practices might be rekindled.

But let me make a few things clear about this resolution. No one *told* me to do this. It wasn't a case of *should* and it certainly wasn't an add-on. I became involved with Native culture because I *wanted* to; I don't think it's overly dramatic to say I *needed* to. This involvement was a function of some of the most basic values I absorbed from my family—values about civil rights and human dignity and solidarity. It wasn't a matter of taking on a "cause." It was a matter of doing what felt right.

For me, the natural way to get involved was through music. But I quickly realized that, if I hoped to have anything of value to give, I first had a lot to learn. In other words, even the *intention* to give back was enough to set the enrichment loop in motion.

I started reading voraciously. I went to the library, found the Native American section, began with the A's, and just kept going. Along the way, I became intrigued with Native languages—not only with their forms and meanings, but with their *cadence*—and how their particular rhythms and phrasing could be set to music.

This, in turn, started me thinking about composing for a choir.

Note that my music-writing career had begun with ten-second "interstitials," then moved on to thirty-second commercials, then to four-minute songs. But now I was making a quantum leap both in scale and in the forces I was writing for. What emboldened me to do this? What gave me the confidence to take on bigger things? It was the fact that I was now dedicating my work to something larger than myself. A larger purpose called for larger music. Again, I was being enriched, getting at least as much as I was giving.

Around this time, through my association with Kevin Costner and the work I'd done on *Dances with Wolves,* I was presented with an extraordinary opportunity: the chance to write eight hours of music for the miniseries *500 Nations.* I'm proud to say that my score was critically acclaimed; but I was even more proud to be associated with a project that acknowledged the variety and importance of Native cultures and that helped create awareness of the present-day realities of Native Americans, both on and off the reservation.

The miniseries ended; my desire to stay involved with Native issues did not. Hoping to build on the momentum of *500 Nations,* I began thinking about a multimedia presentation that would combine music, dance, storytelling, and visuals. Thus was born *Spirit,* which would begin its life as a PBS pledge-break special, then go on to tour as a live theatrical event.

At the outset, however, there were a few small difficulties to overcome. One of these was that I had no idea how to create a live theatrical event! Once again, I was forced to stretch, to learn, to enrich myself in the name of having something to offer back.

By this time, I'd worked for years at the craft of matching sound to image, using music to advance a story. But the story itself had always preexisted; that was someone else's job! Now, for the first time, it was my responsibility—in partnership with some wonderful collaborators—to come up with a narrative framework. To do this, I had to think harder and more systemically than I ever had before about the mechanics and magic of storytelling. I read the great books of Joseph Campbell, *The Power of Myth* and *The Hero with a Thousand Faces,* which stressed the universality of human nature and human yearnings.

Reading Campbell turned out to be one of the formative events of my intellectual life; his passionate respect for story was contagious—and enriching. (I think it's entirely possible that my own desire to write a book someday began with reading his.)

In the near term, reading Campbell provided me with the mythic framework I was looking for: the Hero's journey. Whatever the precise details in a given instance, the journey was always *inward*. Its goal was self-knowledge . . . but that was not an end in itself. Rather, the self-knowledge was a means of *reconnecting* with the world, but at a higher plane of understanding, so that one could serve as a guide to others.

I realized that this was the whole point of the *Spirit* show: reconnection. Not only for the Native peoples who'd weathered a long and bitter campaign aimed at denying them their cultural identity, but for *all* of us who felt alienated from our truest selves. Everyone, I hoped, could feel some uplift in being reminded where they'd come from, who they really were; I felt some of that uplift myself—another instance of gaining by giving.

The *Spirit* show premiered on PBS and did, in fact, go on to tour; the high point, for me, was a performance on the National Mall in Washington, D.C. It would take many pages to explain all the things I learned along the way—everything from stagecraft to the physics of the giant, custom tent in which we performed. But there's another side to all of this that needs to be acknowledged: The experience was also draining and frustrating as hell!

Mounting the show was utterly exhausting. The logistics were daunting from start to finish. Relationships were strained by passionate differences of opinion. Money was lost—both my own, and that of early backers.

I say this not by way of complaint, but to make a point

about this personal kind of giving back. It isn't easy! Nor should it be. Writing a check is easy. But trying to give something back to the world, as a function of one's own energy and convictions and unique set of abilities, is tough. It calls for exactly the kind of commitment that ambitious and hardworking people usually reserve for their day jobs.

But giving back is just as important as taking in. Why should it call for anything less than the same level of effort and determination?

I recently heard a story that provides a striking instance of this intense and hands-on kind of giving back.

In 1990, a journalist friend was asked by a magazine editor to write an article about the former president Jimmy Carter. Carter, in those years, was devoting a lot of time to Habitat for Humanity, an organization that built housing for the homeless as well as for recovering addicts, single-parent families, and other people facing extreme economic challenges. The only way to reach the former president was through Habitat's media office, so my friend called them up and asked if they could arrange an interview.

They were happy to do so, but the offer came at a price. In exchange for the opportunity to interview Carter, the journalist would have to give Habitat one full day of physical labor.

"I agreed, of course," my friend recalls, "but without quite knowing what I was letting myself in for. Then I got a call, instructing me to show up at a certain address in North Philadelphia at eight a.m. on a particular day in August. The former president and first lady would be working on a construction site that day. I would join their crew, and could do the interview when the workday was finished.

"As it turned out," the journalist went on, "it was an absolutely brutal day—a hundred two degrees and humid, with a glaring, hazy sun. I met the others in the crew, the Carters included. We had a brief meeting to introduce ourselves and assign tasks. Since my building skills were zero, my job was to carry things. I carried two-by-fours. I carried Sheetrock. I carried bundles of vinyl siding.

"But the point of the story isn't what *I* did. It's what the Carters did. Call me cynical—I'd expected that the ex-president and first lady would basically be figureheads. I thought they'd show up in work clothes and hammer a symbolic nail or two, then pose for a photo op and retreat to the shade. Jimmy Carter, after all, had been the leader of the free world. He was lending his name and his prestige. Wasn't that enough?

"It turned out that it wasn't *nearly* enough for the Carters, and I have to say I was humbled about my cynicism. The former first couple worked as hard as anyone. Jimmy—that was what he wanted to be called—cut vinyl siding, bending over a long table that held a power saw. Rosalynn took measurements, positioned the siding, and made sure it fit. She wore a big hat for shade, but still, her face was flushed with the heat. The ex-president wore safety goggles that steamed up from the humidity.

"Over the course of the day," my friend remembers, "I chatted with the Carters. But the conversation consisted mostly of things like 'Put that over here' or 'Does that look straight to you?' In other words, the former president was making it clear that this was not about *him*; it was about the task at hand. He wasn't there as a celebrity; he was there as a human being applying his own skill and his own sweat toward a cause he truly believed in.

"We worked till four o'clock, by which point a house had been partly framed and sided, and all of us were thirsty and tired. Then the media liaison came over and asked me if I was ready for the interview. And I realized that I didn't *need* the interview, that the interview, in fact, would be beside the point. What could Carter say, that he hadn't already *shown*? What could I ask him that hadn't already been answered by his actions? The interview would only be words, while the day had been all about deeds.

"So I just shook the ex-president's hand and thanked him for the privilege of working alongside him. Carter replied that doing this work was a privilege for all of us."

• • •

• • •

So then, in the preceding couple of anecdotes, we've unearthed some seeming contradictions about the art of giving back.

My experience with the *Spirit* show taught me that the determination to give back could be tremendously enriching, but that the process could also lead to conflict and frustration.

The Jimmy Carter story makes the point that, even for an ex-president, it's a privilege to do grimy physical labor under miserable heat and glare.

How are we to deal with these paradoxes? I say: Accept them and proceed!

These seeming contradictions are part of the complexity and richness of life. If life is what we make it, and if we want our lives to be as full and textured as possible, we have to find the will to power through them.

Yes, giving of ourselves is a demanding business . . . and also a risky one, an act of self-exposure. Giving of ourselves shows what we are made of, what we *have* to give.

No, there aren't any guarantees that the giving will go smoothly or accomplish all that we hope it will.

What does seem pretty certain is that giving of ourselves will require us to stretch, to venture past our comfort zones and break out of our usual routines.

For that reason, I suppose it's natural to feel a certain

resistance to truly giving of ourselves. I know, because I've experienced that resistance myself.

Some background is in order.

In my family, a clear distinction was drawn between *making money* and *hoarding wealth*. My father, of course, has proved extraordinarily adept at the former, but this was a function of his passion for his work, not of a drive to acquire. Making money was the solid evidence that my father's hunches were correct, that his analyses were sound. It was also the fulfillment of his fiduciary responsibility to his shareholders—by whom he's done pretty well! If other investors wanted to plow their gains into yachts or giant houses or whatever, that was their prerogative, of course. But it had never been my father's plan. My father's plan was to give the wealth back to the world that had produced it in the first place.

Starting just over a decade ago, my siblings and I were recruited into this strategy. At Christmas 1999, our parents endowed our first foundations. The endowments were ten million dollars each—considerable sums to be sure, but manageable. Like every other human undertaking, running a charitable enterprise entails a learning curve. Mistakes, inevitably, get made; it's best to keep those mistakes to a less than calamitous scale!

Over the next several years, as my wife, Jennifer, and I grew more comfortable and practiced in our roles, my parents kept adding funds to the endowment. By the time of my mother's death in 2004, we had stewardship of more than a hundred million dollars.

But let me make a candid admission here: I was extremely ambivalent about all of this, and it was a very lucky thing that Jennifer was not just an active partner, but a thoroughly committed one, because she got stuck with most of the administrative and highly detailed work that went with the foundation.

As for me, I was still wrestling with some fairly basic issues. Remember, I'd been the shy and rather solitary kid who took solace in the piano. My interest in photography had been, in part at least, a way to keep my distance from events—to remain an observer rather than a participant. As some wise man once observed, people don't change, they only become more so; even as an adult then, I loved working alone, communing with the keyboard. I cherished my privacy.

At the same time, I understood that, as my father's son and carrying the Buffett name, I would also feel a tug toward a more public life. The foundation was becoming the machinery that provided the tug—and for a while I resisted it.

I resisted for a simple, selfish, and entirely understandable reason: I was protecting the life I already had. My career in music. My calm routines. My time to read or simply sit still with my wife.

I took great satisfaction from those things. What I

didn't yet realize was that, once I overcame my resistance and threw myself wholeheartedly into the wider world through philanthropy, there would be satisfactions far greater than I could imagine.

Then came the Big Bang.

In June 2006, my father made front pages all over the world by announcing that he was giving away most of his wealth. The headline number was $37 billion to the Bill and Melinda Gates Foundation. My siblings and I were footnotes to the story at a billion dollars each for our foundations!

Along with my brother and sister, I'd been tipped off to the plan a couple months earlier. My first reaction had been to call my father on the phone and tell him I was really proud of him. It was the only thing I could think of to say.

Only gradually—*very* gradually—did the implications of my father's generosity really sink in. Jennifer and I now had stewardship over a quite significant amount of money. What should we do with it? Was it wiser to support many causes or really to focus on one or two? If the latter, how did we choose? How did we put *ourselves* into the giving, rather than simply distributing cash? How could we maximize the help we were able to give? It was all extremely dizzying!

Now, bear with me a moment, because I want to tell you about a certain knack my father has. Sometimes, in the midst of a conversation, my father will segue into something that seems only tangentially related. This may seem puzzling to the listener, but it generally turns out that the segue was completely logical; it's just that my father drew a connection that the other person hadn't yet seen.

It happened that, before the public announcement of my father's gift, the family gathered in Omaha, then flew together to New York. During the plane ride, I was telling my dad about my quandaries regarding the foundation; out of the blue, he asked if I thought the foundation work would have an effect on my music.

I thought it was an odd question, especially since my father left it so open-ended. Was he asking if the foundation would take time and attention away from my composing? Or was he suggesting that the foundation work might actually add something to the creative process? I said vaguely that I didn't see how or why one thing would affect the other.

But of course the foundation work has had an impact on my music! How could it not? My father seemed to recognize that before I did.

Meanwhile, in the months following the Big Bang, Jennifer and I thought long and hard about a mission and a focus for our foundation. We'd named it NoVo, from the Latin word for "change, alter, or invent." But what sort of change did we most hope to see in the world? What strategies could we invent or adopt to help that change along?

After lots of soul-searching and many meetings with more experienced donors and administrators, we defined a few guiding principles for our work. First, we wanted to avoid what I think of as "philanthropic colonialism." This is the tendency of (generally) well-meaning outsiders to imagine that they understand the challenges facing local peoples better than the local people themselves. Imagining that they better understand the problems, they further imagine that they can effectively impose solutions. Not only is this arrogant and condescending, but it usually doesn't work. So our approach would be to provide support for people who identified *their own* needs and evolved *their own* solutions.

Second, we wanted to adapt a long-standing business principle of my father's: investing in undervalued assets. The idea is elegantly simple: Find something the world underappreciates, support it, don't meddle, and allow time for the world to catch up in its valuation.

And when we started thinking about which human assets have been undervalued in many places all around the world, we came up with an answer that was both obvious and shocking: girls. The sad truth is that female children are the victims of inequality in many different cultures. Sons go to school; daughters, often, are barred from doing so. Boys are given opportunities to experience a wider world; girls, too often, remain prisoners of their families and, later, their husbands. We hoped to do something to address these inequalities.

Additionally, we saw a wonderful "multiplier effect" in this approach. Today's girls are tomorrow's mothers. If we could help to promote better health, better education, and more economic independence among young girls, those benefits would be passed on to future generations. The gift would keep on giving.

One of the first initiatives we supported was centered in the West African nations of Liberia and Sierra Leone. We helped provide funding for schools that provided a safe haven for girls and that combined general education with some very practical training. The girls learned to read and write; they also learned to sew—on treadle machines that did not require electricity. Then again, if some of the young women turned out to be electricians, that would be a happy outcome also! The whole idea was to foster a wider range of options. Able to support themselves financially, and to keep their own accounts, these women could look forward to a future of independence and the self-respect that went with it.

This initiative was the occasion for my first trip to Africa, and for me it was a profound experience. I had never seen such a dramatic contrast between material poverty and, on the other hand, a wealth of joy and hope and community. It shamed me, as a Westerner, that we had so much, yet tended to fill our lives with petty anxieties and complaints, while many of the Africans I met, for whom even the basics of food and shelter were not to be taken for granted, faced life with serenity, courage, and humor. What could be done to bridge, even slightly, the unconscionable gap in material circumstances? Equally important, what might we in the West have to learn from societies that were centered on community rather than self-advancement, spiritual wholeness rather than relentless ambition?

Back home, I tried to process the complex emotions of the trip. So what did I do? I sat down at the piano and wrote a song. *Of course* that's what I did! Hadn't I *always* turned to the keyboard when trying to express thoughts and feelings that somehow slipped between the meanings offered by words? It was a lot like playing "Yankee Doodle" in a minor key, back when I was seven! I had something on my mind and in my heart. Music was the way to get it out.

My father's question that had seemed to be a non sequitur, then, had turned out to be a prophecy. My music life and my foundation work were well on the way to weaving thoroughly together, becoming ever more entwined, like strands of DNA.

Shortly after this, I was introduced to an artist named Akon. To be candid, I hadn't heard of him; this was an instance of our own culture being quite provincial in certain ways, since in many places around the world, Akon was already a major pop star. He had heard my song about the Liberia experience, and he'd asked me to send it to him. He ended up remixing the track, and singing on it as well.

Thus was born an alliance in music and activism that is still, I hope, in its early stages. In 2009, Akon and I sang together on another song I'd written and had the honor of performing at the General Assembly of the United Nations.

So here I find myself, at fifty, living a life filled with more resonant satisfactions than I might ever have imagined. Like every life, mine has had both a unity and an evolution. I'm the same person I was at ten or thirty, but over time, my focus has gradually shifted *outward*. As I've grown older, I think less about what *I* need, because the difficult and crucial work of youth has been largely—never entirely!—accomplished. I have found my calling and committed to it. I have proven what I needed to prove, mainly to myself. My emphasis now is to continue pushing back the boundaries, both musical and philanthropic, to keep growing so that I might have more to give.

To be honest, I'm proud of the life I've made. My pride is tempered by gratitude, by a wholehearted acknowledgment of how fortunate I have been. Still, every life has its challenges; one of mine, as I said at the outset, has been to make the best of a good situation. I think I've done an okay job at that.

But let me be clear: I believe that *all* of us should be proud of our lives, because making a life is the one profound and sacred opportunity shared by every person ever born. *Life is what we make it.* No one else can do it for us; no one has the right to tell us what it ought to be.

We make our own goals. We define our own successes. We don't get to choose where we start in life; we *do* get to choose the kind of people we become.

Epilogue

Begin it now

Here is a quote I have always loved. It has been attributed to the great German poet Goethe, though without definitive proof of authorship. Be that as it may, this brief passage touches on something I deeply believe, and neatly encapsulates much of what I have been saying in these pages.

> *Until one is committed, there is hesitancy, the chance to draw back. Concerning all acts of initiative and creation, there is one elementary truth, the ignorance of which kills countless ideas and splendid plans: that the moment one definitely commits oneself, then Providence moves too. All sorts of things occur to help one that would never otherwise have occurred. A whole stream of*

> *events issues from the decision, raising in one's favor all manner of unforeseen incidents and meetings and material assistance, which no man could have dreamed would come his way. Whatever you can do, or dream you can do, begin it. Boldness has genius, power, and magic in it. Begin it now.*

Why do I love this quote? In large part, because of the emphasis it places on *commitment*.

The power and the magic that the passage refers to—where do they come from? *Not* from exceptional talent or exceptional intelligence or exceptional *anything*. The source of the power, rather, is something of which *all of us* are capable, part of our shared stock of human potential—the ability to commit to a vocation, to choose a path, and to forge ahead with determination and patience.

What about the "Providence" mentioned in the quote? As should be clear by now, I personally do not subscribe to any particular religious orthodoxy, and I am leery of any viewpoint that honors one belief system above all others. So let me put my own metaphorical spin on this notion of Providence.

I see it not as a separate force that exists *outside* of us, but rather as the unsuspected reserves of strength and courage and intuition that exist *within* us—and that come to full flower only when we commit and focus with all our hearts.

We have all heard stories about mothers lifting cars to free trapped children, and earthquake victims holding up roofs so that their loved ones might escape. No one who lived through 9/11 will ever forget the spectacle of firefighters streaming into the burning buildings even as the panicked civilians were racing out. Clearly, these are extraordinary acts in extraordinary circumstances, but I believe they point to a few basic and redemptive truths that apply, as well, to the more everyday conduct of life:

We are stronger than we think we are.
We have courage that we do not recognize until we need it.
We are equal to challenges that we haven't even imagined yet.

What is it that allows us to tap into these reserves of strength and nerve—that allows us to discover what is best in ourselves?

Commitment, boldness, and the determination to shape our own lives.

As these words are being written, the global economy is in a state of profound and worrying uncertainty. Unemployment is high; homeowners are facing foreclosure and companies are entering bankruptcy; entire industries are contracting or being rendered obsolete. Older people fear for their pensions and their retirement nest eggs; young people look ahead at a future that seems full of obstacles and hazards.

Perhaps, by the time you read this book, economic prospects will be brighter. But maybe not. No one seems to know. *I* certainly don't. Even my father, legendary for his insight and commonsense straight talk about financial matters, has candidly and publicly acknowledged being buffaloed this time. Seems that no one has ever seen anything exactly like what we've been going through.

I mention these economic challenges not to wallow in doom and gloom. On the contrary, I happen to believe that these baffling times constitute a difficult but wonderful opportunity.

As certain comfortable assumptions seem to be breaking down, we are forced to look at the world—and our own possibilities—with fresh eyes. What if certain "safe" career choices are not so safe after all? What if we can't assume that we will make more money this year than last year, that we will automatically be richer at fifty than at thirty? What if we dare to admit that "job security," while a comforting idea, is often an illusion?

In April 2009, the *New York Times* ran an article entitled "Is This the Time to Chase a Career Dream?" The writer, a career consultant named Pamela Slim, observed that many if not most people had a sort of fantasy career in addition to their actual work. In many cases, not surprisingly, the fantasy career was better-paying and more prestigious than the real job. But there were also many instances in which a quite different dynamic pertained.

People daydreamed not about more money, but more freedom. Not more power, but less stress. Not higher status, but more creative satisfaction. An information technology project manager dreamed of leading hiking expeditions. A successful entrepreneur fantasized about being a driver for United Parcel Service; he longed for order, consistency, exercise, a clear set of tasks to fulfill each working day.

What was going on here? In my view, these surprising "dream jobs" represent a liberation from standard thinking and conventional biases, a healthy return to the basic childhood question as to what we'd like to do when we grow up.

And that begs another simple question: Why *not* do what we like?

I'm not talking about frivolous choices, or self-indulgent choices, or lazy choices.

I *am* talking about choices that reflect our own *personal* values, and that give the broadest possible scope to our particular talents and creativity.

If you are drawn to music, or painting, or writing, why not go for it?

If teaching seems to offer you fulfillment, why not choose that path?

If you are drawn to outdoor work far from the centers of commerce and wealth, why not go there?

There are, of course, some pretty powerful "why nots" to be considered when making these sorts of unconventional choices. Careers in the arts are notoriously uncertain. Work in the helping professions like teaching and nursing does not tend to be rewarded with either the money or the status it deserves. Removing oneself from the action of the major cities requires a certain kind of self-reliance.

On top of that, it seems to be a fact of human nature that, when economic times are tough, people get more cautious, more constrained in the choices they allow themselves.

This caution is understandable, I guess. But think about it: Shouldn't just the opposite be true?

If even the most conventional M.B.A. career paths are strewn with hazards and pitfalls, isn't that a reason to allow oneself a wider range of choices?

If a certain money-based version of "success" has been tarnished, isn't that an opportunity to define for ourselves a more humane and encompassing notion of success?

If ever-increasing material wealth can no longer be taken for granted, doesn't it make sense to place a greater emphasis on the sort of wealth that is measured in personal fulfillment and peace of mind?

• • •

This is a very personal book, so let me end it on a personal note.

As I've said from the start, I make no claim of special expertise in the conduct of life, still less in the mystery of life's meaning. It is not my ambition to be seen as a counselor. Here and there in these pages, I do presume to offer advice, and I make no apology for that. There are certain things I passionately believe to be true. Where I can make a case for those truths, where I think I can provide some clarity and perspective, I have not been shy about doing so.

But, from my own point of view, offering advice to you, the reader, is only a small part of what this book has been about. First and foremost, this book has been a way for me to think out loud.

"The unexamined life is not worth living." Plato wrote that, and it's only become more true in the two and a half millennia between his time and ours. Life moves faster and faster; it grows more and more filled with distractions. As clutter builds up at the periphery—cell phones, instant messages, the unremitting bombardment of the media—it becomes ever more challenging to filter out the noise, to remember where the center is. This book has given me the opportunity to sit quietly and enjoy the great luxury of some quality time in and around that center.

What have I found there?

Most basically of all, I've found gratitude.

Gratitude to my mother, for her life lessons in tolerance, trust, and boundless curiosity about other human beings. Gratitude to my father, for his example of self-discipline, hard work, and tireless pursuit of a destiny chosen by himself. Gratitude to my wife, for her true partnership in all the things that matter to us as we continue to grow as individuals.

I've discovered a heightened gratitude, too, for music. I've always loved music, of course; now I see it as nothing short of a miracle. That certain tones and rhythms can provide solace and joy, can break down barriers between people and say things that words cannot—this is amazing! To participate in the miracle of music as a composer and performer has been, and remains, an enormous privilege.

Not everything I've discovered at the center of my thoughts has been quite so pleasant, of course. Looking back at my younger self, I've found much to scratch my head about.

Might I have made more of my opportunities in formal education? Why did it take me as long as it did to embrace my musical calling? Why did I let my insecurities control me at this or that juncture? Why, even as a so-called adult, did I make certain blunders that, in retrospect, seem obvious and avoidable?

I have no airtight answers to these questions. But the

writing of this book has provided me with a useful framework for considering them. Considering them *calmly*, without excuses or embarrassment, without the corrosive residue of guilt that often attaches to mistakes we *don't* admit. I can't undo my errors; I can't disown them. What I *have* been able to do is learn from them, to accept them as part of the mix of things that have made my life uniquely my own.

But mistakes are one thing; regrets are another. Mistakes happen and generally are over with. Regrets linger. A mistake is an event. Regret is atmospheric.

It's fashionable, I think, to deny having any regrets, to claim that, if one could live life over again, one wouldn't change a thing. Frankly, I think this is boastful nonsense, or maybe just symptomatic of a life that *hasn't* been examined. Over the course of years and decades, regrets both small and large tend to accumulate. How could they not, given how many choices we face each day, how many times we are challenged to rise to an occasion? Regrets are nothing more or less than evidence of having lived; they're like the little scrapes and scars that line our knees and elbows. The good news is that after a while they don't hurt anymore; but it's dishonest to pretend they aren't there.

When I think about my own regrets, a subtle but persistent pattern emerges: My regrets cluster around those moments when I failed to heed the advice of the Goethe quote with which I began this epilogue.

I regret my hesitations.

I regret the times I sold short the mysterious power of *commitment itself.*

Commitment moves the world. It both powers and heals us; it's fuel and medicine together. It's the antidote to regret, to apathy, to lack of self-belief. Commitment batters down closed doors and levels bumpy roads. Commitment begets confidence and also *justifies* confidence. Commitment enlarges our efforts by drawing on those deep-down resources that lie fallow until we determine to discover them and use them.

So, in closing, I will say to you the same thing I have said to myself a thousand times:

Your life is yours to create. Be grateful for the opportunity. Seize it with passion and boldness. Whatever you decide to do, *commit* to it with all your strength . . . and begin it now.

What are you waiting for?

Acknowledgments

I would like to thank Laurence Shames, a tremendous editor and writer who became a good friend, for his invaluable contributions, Richard Pine for his guidance, Lydia Loizides for the idea, and John Glusman for believing in it.

Thank you to those who have helped make my life what it is: my parents, my grandparents Bill and Dorothy Thompson, Howie and Susie Buffett, Pam Buffett, Tom Rogers, Letha Clark, Kent Bellows, Lars Erickson, Layne Yahnke, Frankie Pane, Bill Buffett, Erica and Nicole Buffett, my wife, Jennifer—and everyone who has, continues to, or will provide life's lessons.

About the Author

Emmy Award–winning musician Peter Buffett has an acclaimed career that spans more than twenty-eight years as a professional songwriter, producer, performer, and composer for film and television. He is the musical mind behind many of the early MTV bumpers of the 1980s and the climactic crescendo in the memorable "Firedance" scene in 1990's Oscar-winning film *Dances with Wolves.*

Buffett has received critical acclaim for his Native American–inspired music, most notably composing the full score for *500 Nations*—the eight-hour Emmy-awarded CBS miniseries produced by Kevin Costner, and the musical production *Spirit: The Seventh Fire*—a Native American–inspired show incorporating live native dancing, powwow singing, and IMAX-scale visuals (which premiered on the National Mall as part of the opening of the Smithsonian's National Museum of the American Indian in Washington, D.C.).

Buffett began experimenting with vocals and a more eclectic pop/rock sound in recent years. His latest work combines elements of soft and progressive rock in the vein of Simon and Garfunkel and Beck.

Buffett has collaborated with Grammy-nominated recording artist Akon to release two human-rights inspired songs, one of which debuted at a special event at the UN General Assembly. He is also the only man to have performed at Eve Ensler's Tenth Anniversary V-Day celebration in New Orleans.

For more information, please visit www.peterbuffett.com.